YORK NOTES

CW00684425

WUTHERING HEIGHTS

EMILY BRONTË

Notes by Claire Steele

PEARSON

YORK PRESS

YORK PRESS
322 Old Brompton Road, London SW5 9JH

PEARSON EDUCATION LIMITED
Edinburgh Gate, Harlow,
Essex CM20 2JE, United Kingdom

Associated companies, branches and representatives throughout the world

First published 1998
New editions 2004, 2012
This new and fully revised edition 2016

10 9 8 7 6 5 4 3 2

ISBN 978–1–2921–3819–0

Illustration on page 61 by Alan Batley

Phototypeset by Carnegie Book Production
Printed in Slovakia

Photo credits: Alamy Stock Image/Alamy for page 6 / sy33/Shutterstock for page 7 / Steven Chiang/Shutterstock for page 8 / © iStock/Lisa-Blue for page 9 / Brian A Jackson/Shutterstock for page 10 middle / © iStock/imageoRB for page 10 bottom / Stephen Street/Alamy for page 11 / Oleg Golovnev/Shutterstock for page 12 top / © iStock/Lisa-Blue for page 12 bottom / LiliGraphie/Shutterstock for page 13 top / ruigsantos/Shutterstock for page 13 middle / revers/Shutterstock for page 14 / Mila Supinskaya/Shutterstock for page 15 / Igor Zh/Shutterstock for page 16 / Anneka/Shutterstock for page 17 / The National Trust Photo Library/Alamy for page 19 top / Ken Felepchuk/Shutterstock for page 19 bottom / The National Trust Photolibrary/Alamy for page 20 / Yuri Tuchkov/Shutterstock for page 21 / WIN-IniativeNeleman/Getty for page 22 / Kanea/Shutterstock for page 23 / Radoslaw Maciejewski/Shutterstock for page 24 / © iStock/Arturo Limon for page 25 top / Andrew Roland/Shutterstock for page 25 bottom / Mrlee1989/Shutterstock for page 26 / Anna Tamila/Shutterstock for page 27 / © iStock/Chris Warren for page 28 / gemphoto/Shutterstock for page 29 / andamanec/Shutterstock for page 30 / Ioskutnikov/Shutterstock for page 31 / Fribus Mara/Shutterstock for page 32 / Betsie Van der Meer/Getty for page 34 top / merc67/Thinkstock for page 34 bottom / Palmer Kane LLC/Shutterstock for page 35 / Smileus/Shutterstock for page 36 / FotograFFF/Shutterstock for page 37 / g-stockstudio/Shutterstock for page 38 / e2dan/Shutterstock for page 39 / © iStock/spxChrome for page 40 / © iStock/GavinD for page 41 / stocker1970/Shutterstock for page 42 / © iStock/Shelly Perry for page 43 / Anneka/Shutterstock for page 44 / Zena Holloway/Getty for page 45 / Maryna Kulchytska/Shutterstock for page 46 / © iStock/StephanieFrey for page 47 / Glenkar/Shutterstock for page 48 / Roman Pavlik/Shutterstock for page 49 / © iStock/Ida Jarosova for page 50 / kai keisuke/Shutterstock for page 51 / © iStock/robynmac for page 52 / © iStock/Marilyn Nieves for page 53 / Juan Moyano/Thinkstock for page 54 / Sebastian Crocker/Shutterstock for page 55 / © iStock/chris2766 for page 56 / © iStock/Kerstin Waurick for page 57 / Gregory Costanzo/Getty for page 58 / Lario Tus/Shutterstock for page 59 / Anneka/Shutterstock for page 62 top / arka38/Shutterstock for page 62 bottom / WIN-IniativeNeleman/Getty for page 63 / Kuttelvaserova Stuchelova/Shutterstock for page 64 top / Mark Medcalf/Shutterstock for page 64 bottom / Betsie Van der Meer/Getty for page 65 top / © iStock/Edgaras Marozas for page 65 bottom / exopixel/Shutterstock for page 66 top / © iStock/GlobalP for page 66 bottom / Ruslan Kokarev/Shutterstock for page 67 / Zena Holloway/Getty for page 68 top / Juan Moyano/Thinkstock for page 68 bottom / Fribus Mara/Shutterstock for page 69 / Gregory Costanzo/Getty for page 70 top / Ysbran d Cosijn/Shutterstock for page 70 bottom / Elena Schweitzer/Shutterstock for page 71 / 1000 words/Shutterstock for page 73 / donatas1/Shutterstock for page 74 / © iStock/Michael Luhrenberg for page 77 / © iStock/Maciej Laska for page 78 / samzsolti/Shutterstock for page 80 / Bork/Shutterstock for page 81 / Neil Burton/Shutterstock for page 82 bottom left / LarisaR/Shutterstock for page 82 bottom right / World History Archive/Alamy for page 84 / ASC Photography/Shutterstock for page 84 / Everett-Art/Shutterstock for page 86 top / DEA Picture Library/Getty for page 86 bottom / Lebrecht Music and Arts Photo Library/Alamy for page 87 bottom right / Granger, NYC/Alamy for page 87 bottom left / studiovin/Shutterstock for page 88 / Kerry Dunstone/Alamy for page 89 / olemac/Thinkstock for page 91 / © iStock/gremlin for page 92 top / neftali/Shutterstock for page 92 bottom / The Print Collector/Alamy for page 93 / zakalinka/Shutterstock for page 94

CONTENTS

PART FIVE: CONTEXTS AND INTERPRETATIONS

PART SIX: PROGRESS BOOSTER

PART SEVEN: FURTHER STUDY AND ANSWERS

HOW TO USE YOUR YORK NOTES TO STUDY AND REVISE *WUTHERING HEIGHTS*

These Notes can be used in a range of ways to help you read, study and revise for your exam or assessment.

Become an informed and independent reader

Throughout the Notes, you will find the following key features to aid your study:

- **'Key context'** margin features: these widen your knowledge of the setting, whether historical, social or political. This is highlighted by the AO3 (Assessment Objective 3) symbol to remind you of its connection to aspects you may want to refer to in your exam responses.
- **'Key interpretation'** boxes (a key part of AO5): do you agree with the perspective or idea that is explained here? Does it help you form your own view on events or characters? Developing your own interpretations is a key element of higher-level achievement in A Level, so make use of this and similar features.
- **'Key connection'** features (linked to AO4): whether or not you refer to such connections in your exam writing, having a wider understanding of how the novel, or aspects of it, links to other texts or ideas can give you new perspectives on the text.
- **'Study focus'** panels: these help to secure your own understanding of key elements of the text. Being able to write in depth on a particular point or explain a specific feature will help your writing sound professional and informed.
- **'Key quotation'** features: these identify the effect of specific language choices – you could use these for revision purposes at a later date.
- **'Progress booster'** features: these offer specific advice about how to tackle a particular aspect of your study, or an idea you might want to consider discussing in your exam responses.
- **'Extract analysis'** sections: these are vital for you to use either during your reading or when you come back to the text afterwards. These sections take a core extract from a chapter and explore it in real depth, explaining its significance and impact, raising questions and offering interpretations.

Stay on track with your study and revision

Your first port of call will always be your teacher, and you should already have a good sense of how well you are doing, but the Notes offer you several ways of measuring your progress.

- **'Revision task'**: throughout the Notes, there are some challenging, but achievable, written tasks for you to do relevant to the section just covered. Suggested answers are supplied in **Part Seven**.
- **'Progress check'**: this feature comes at the end of **Parts Two** to **Five**, and contains a range of short and longer tasks which address key aspects of the Part of the Notes you have just read. Below this is a grid of key skills which you can complete to track your progress, and rate your understanding.
- **'Practice task'** and **'Mark scheme'**: use these features to make a judgement on how well you know the text and how well you can apply the skills you have learned.

Most importantly, enjoy using these Notes and see your knowledge and skills improve.

The edition used in these Notes is the Penguin Classics edition, 2003.

 PROGRESS BOOSTER

You can choose to use the Notes as you wish, but as you read the novel it can be useful to read over the **Part Two** summaries and analysis in order to embed key events, ideas and developments in the **narrative**.

 PROGRESS BOOSTER

Don't forget to make full use of **Parts Three** to **Five** of the Notes during your reading of the novel. You may have essays to complete on **genre**, or key **themes**, or on the impact of specific settings, and can therefore make use of these in-depth sections. Or you may simply want to check out a particular idea or area as you're reading or studying the novel in class.

 PROGRESS BOOSTER

Part Six: Progress booster will introduce you to different styles of question and how to tackle them; help you to improve your expression so that it has a suitably academic and professional tone; assist you with planning and use of evidence to support ideas; and, most importantly, show you three sample exam responses at different levels with helpful AO-related annotations and follow-up comments. Dedicating time to working through this Part will be something you won't regret.

WUTHERING HEIGHTS: A SNAPSHOT

Why is *Wuthering Heights* still studied and enjoyed today?

Wuthering Heights is a remarkable novel, deeply passionate, complex, challenging and stylistically ground-breaking. Its rewards are multiple and emerge from patient, close reading. This is a novel that takes the love story as its central **theme** and turns it into something thrilling, dark, disturbing and life-changing. This is not a romantic love story. It is the story of obsession, fatal attraction and a haunting, destructive love. Brontë's story has prompted many film and theatre adaptations, but arguably it is best suited to the form of the novel, the form that permits all its multiple layers and contradictions, and gives sufficient space for its astonishing fullness and subtlety. Brontë reinvents the novel in *Wuthering Heights*, investing it with a wild, potent energy that remains with you long after you close the book.

Wuthering Heights: A woman's place in literature

Wuthering Heights is Emily Brontë's only novel and it was published together with her sister Anne's novel *Agnes Grey* in December 1847. The sisters decided to use the same deliberately masculine-sounding **pseudonyms** they had used a year earlier when they published their book of poetry under the title *Poems by Currer, Ellis and Acton Bell*. This was because, as women writers, they wanted their poetry to receive due critical attention.

As their elder sister Charlotte Brontë explained: 'we had a vague impression that authoresses are liable to be looked on with prejudice' (Biographical Notice in *Wuthering Heights*, p. xliv). The identity of the authors was only revealed by Charlotte when she revised the text of *Wuthering Heights* and added her preface to the second edition, published in 1850, two years after Emily Brontë's death. Most modern editions of the novel include Charlotte Brontë's prefaces.

The Brontë sisters were right to be concerned: some readers reacted negatively to Charlotte's revelation that Ellis Bell, the author of *Wuthering Heights*, was in fact a woman. Some of these prejudices appear clearly in the letters between Charlotte Brontë and the famous poet Robert Southey, who wrote: 'Literature cannot be the business of a woman's life, and it ought not to be.' It is possible to argue therefore that *Wuthering Heights* challenged both Victorian ideas about what was proper for literature and what was proper for a woman.

The Gothic genre

Wuthering Heights has been described as a **Gothic** novel, a style of literature which combines horror and romance. It typically features supernatural encounters, graveyards, ghosts, desolate landscapes and crumbling ruins in order to convey the effect of pleasurable terror. The Gothic was a form of literature popular in the late eighteenth and nineteenth centuries, and generally dealt with the supernatural and the fantastic.

Haunted by ghosts and hallucinations, *Wuthering Heights* fits neatly with the supernatural traits of the Gothic. Heathcliff's profound passion and desire for Catherine, which extends beyond the grave and **transcends** the conventional boundaries of class and time, clearly places Gothic ideas at the heart of Brontë's novel. Its idiosyncratic form and sensitivity to social realities, however, move beyond conventional descriptions of the Gothic novel. It is a provoking text, full of contradictions, which defies stable readings and is full of unresolved puzzles, unexplained dreams and unquiet ghosts.

Social context

It is important to consider the social context of the novel, at the time when it was written. Contemporary readers of *Wuthering Heights* would have been familiar with stories like that of Heathcliff being a foundling from the port of Liverpool. Orphans and child beggars were a common social problem. Heathcliff's uncertain origins can be read as a realistic account of the social upheavals of the mid nineteenth century, which saw mass unemployment as a result of the Industrial Revolution, and the decay of a rural lifestyle in the face of increased urbanisation and new technology.

The Industrial Revolution dramatically changed the social structure in Britain. Prior to industrialisation, three quarters of Britain's population lived in the countryside, working in agriculture or as skilled craftsmen. The new enclosure laws of 1845–82 meant that many farmers could no longer afford to farm the land. The factories were capable of producing far more, and far more quickly, than a hand-weaver. This meant that families were forced to move to the towns to work in the factories, where they toiled for long hours and were paid very little money. Family life was eroded, people could no longer sustain themselves, and there was widespread poverty and unrest.

A02

Study focus: Key issues to explore

As you study the text and revise for the exam, keep in mind these key elements and ideas:

- Language: who uses it and how? This is a novel which explores many different registers of language from the colloquial to the poetic.
- The role of identity and how it is constantly under revision in the novel, as different generations bear the same names.
- The conflict between culture and nature and how this forms the structural spine of the novel. It is broadly represented by the two houses, Thrushcross Grange and Wuthering Heights respectively.
- The theme of transgression and authenticity: what is proper behaviour within the novel, and how do the characters keep true to themselves?
- The role of women and how their characters and roles are shaped by social contexts.
- Love and all its different forms.
- The supernatural: how do the uncanny and religion operate in this novel to expand on what love might mean?

- Family: how loyalty and family structures are interrogated through violence, jealousy, pride, betrayal and belonging.
- Revenge and its key role in driving the plot forwards.

In each case, make sure you develop your own interpretations and, with the help of these Notes, prepare to argue your viewpoint on them.

SYNOPSIS

The beginning

The novel famously opens with the date 1801, suggesting both a new beginning and a diary entry. The **narrator**, Mr Lockwood, is visiting Yorkshire and is the new tenant of Thrushcross Grange. His landlord, who lives at Wuthering Heights, is Heathcliff, described by Lockwood as 'a dark-skinned gypsy in aspect, in dress and manners a gentleman' (Vol. I, Ch. I, p. 5). We are offered a description of the threshold of Wuthering Heights, bearing the date 1500 and the name Hareton Earnshaw, but the history of the property is postponed as Lockwood is intimidated by the surliness of his landlord. In spite of a hostile welcome and an evident lack of desire on Heathcliff's part for the visit to be repeated, Lockwood nevertheless closes the chapter with a vow to return the following day.

The first three chapters detail Lockwood's relationship with his landlord, Heathcliff, and his experience of a sequence of vivid and inexplicable dreams in Heathcliff's home, Wuthering Heights. The **narrative** then passes to Nelly Dean, who takes us back in time to Heathcliff's arrival at the Heights as a child.

Childhood

Catherine and Heathcliff grow up as siblings, after Heathcliff is introduced into the Earnshaw household by Catherine's father as a foundling and given the name of a dead son. Their relationship is intense and exclusive: '[Catherine] was much too fond of Heathcliff. The greatest punishment we could invent for her was to keep her separate from him' (Vol. I, Ch. V, p. 42). When their father dies, Catherine's brother Hindley returns to Wuthering Heights with a wife, Frances, and becomes the master of the house. Hindley's wish to sever the intimacy between Catherine and Heathcliff is aided by Catherine spending five weeks at the neighbouring house, Thrushcross Grange, following a foot injury caused by the owners' guard dog. Catherine returns to the Heights transformed into a lady, having made friends with the children of the Grange – Edgar and Isabella. While Catherine has been away, Hindley has systematically degraded Heathcliff, refusing him education and insisting that he work as a labourer on the grounds. Hindley and Frances have a son, Hareton, and shortly afterwards Frances dies.

Marriage

Following Catherine's decision to marry Edgar, Heathcliff disappears for three years, and Catherine moves to Thrushcross Grange. Her marriage to Edgar is described as affectionate, if subdued. In other words it conforms to the conventions of marriage in the nineteenth century. It is a marriage typified by a kind of quiet friendliness, and as such it is utterly at odds with what we have previously seen of Catherine's character.

Nelly Dean, the housekeeper, moves with Catherine from the Heights. When Heathcliff returns he has become an imposing and compelling figure of a man. He enraptures Catherine, and captivates Isabella, much to the annoyance of Edgar.

Heathcliff and Isabella

Heathcliff stays at Wuthering Heights, with his former enemy Hindley, whom he engages in gambling and drinking. In spite of multiple warnings, Isabella falls in love with Heathcliff, who sees that she might well be his route to wreaking revenge upon Edgar for depriving him of Catherine.

Edgar and Heathcliff argue violently, which makes Catherine ill. Heathcliff courts Isabella. Isabella and Heathcliff elope and Edgar disowns his sister as a result.

For two months Edgar nurses Catherine, and there is no word from Isabella or Heathcliff. Then a letter from Isabella to Nelly Dean reveals that they are back at Wuthering Heights, and that the marriage is desperately unhappy. Isabella begs Nelly to visit her at the Heights, which she does. Heathcliff makes a passionate declaration of his love for Catherine, and an equally powerful vilification of Isabella. Nelly berates him for his treatment of Isabella, but in the end relents and carries a letter from him to deliver to Catherine. This marks the end of the first volume.

The next generation

Volume II commences with Heathcliff visiting Catherine. He sees that her death is both imminent and inevitable. She dies that evening, giving birth prematurely to a daughter, Cathy.

Isabella flees from Heathcliff and her oppressive marriage, and moves to the south of England, where a few months later she gives birth to a son, Linton Heathcliff. At about this time Hindley dies, leaving Heathcliff alone at the Heights with Hareton, whom Heathcliff treats as badly as Hindley had treated Heathcliff in the past. When Isabella dies, Linton, now twelve and a sickly, effeminate child, is taken to Thrushcross Grange by Edgar. Heathcliff sends for him and he returns to Wuthering Heights to live with his father.

Young Cathy lives in cherished seclusion at Thrushcross Grange, unaware that her cousin Linton is now living at the Heights. On her sixteenth birthday, however, she meets Heathcliff and Hareton by chance on the moors and returns with them to Wuthering Heights where she is astonished to see Linton.

Heathcliff plans that Cathy and Linton should marry, for then he can gain control of both houses. Linton is sick and irritable, but Cathy's generosity commits her to making his life happier, a generosity which Heathcliff exploits fully. Cathy is forbidden by Edgar to return to the Heights, but contrives to write to Linton instead. Eventually, she gets the opportunity to pay him visits undetected by either Edgar or Nelly Dean. Heathcliff's plan that the two cousins should marry is under time pressure, because of Linton's ill health. Heathcliff's obsession with revenge drives him to tyranny. Eventually he forces a marriage between the two, since he is unable to manipulate events in any other way.

Edgar dies, and Thrushcross Grange passes to Linton as the only son of Isabella, rather than to Cathy, the daughter of Edgar. When Linton dies soon afterwards, Heathcliff claims inheritance of Thrushcross Grange, since Cathy is now his daughter-in-law. Thus cruelly dispossessed, Cathy lives in miserable seclusion at the Heights. This brings us to the point at which Lockwood arrives as tenant of Thrushcross Grange, and introduces himself into the household.

The final three chapters of the second volume, mirroring the first three of the first, restore the narrative to Lockwood, who returns to the Heights a year later, to find that Heathcliff has died and Cathy and Hareton are enjoying a blissful courtship prior to their impending marriage.

A05 **KEY INTERPRETATION**

In his 1926 essay 'The Structure of "Wuthering Heights"', C. P. Sanger makes a detailed examination of the legal aspects of *Wuthering Heights* and identifies the complex strategic route by which Heathcliff takes possession of both the Heights and Thrushcross Grange.

A03 **KEY CONTEXT**

Brontë's understanding of the intricacies of nineteenth-century property law is evident from the complex plot structure of *Wuthering Heights*. In the nineteenth century there was a fundamental difference between the law of the land (property) and that of goods and money (personal property). The law of the land was such that males had preference over females. Males inherited according to seniority of birth and took precedence over females in terms of inheritance rights.

VOLUME I, CHAPTER I

Summary

- It is the year 1801. While staying in Yorkshire, Mr Lockwood pays his landlord, Heathcliff, a somewhat unwelcome visit.
- We are also introduced to Heathcliff's servant Joseph and a female servant.

Analysis

KEY CONNECTION **A04**

'I "never told my love"' (Vol. I, Ch. I, p. 6) is a reference to Shakespeare's *Twelfth Night* (Act II, Scene 4, lines 114–16), establishing Lockwood as an educated narrator.

Study focus: The narrators **A02**

The chapter opens with Lockwood, an outsider, coming into a world which he finds hostile and unnerving. Recounting his visit to Wuthering Heights, and his meeting with Heathcliff, Lockwood is established as an unreliable and vain **narrator**: 'I felt interested in a man who seemed more exaggeratedly reserved than myself' (Vol. I, Ch. I, p. 3).

Time

As some critics, most notably C. P. Sanger, have noted, Brontë pays careful attention to time. Although the exact date is only given on three occasions, there are many markers, such as seasonal references and ages of characters, which alert us to the complex time shifts in the novel. The importance of chronological exactitude is established when the first chapter begins with the date: 1801. This date, which is suggestive of a diary entry, grounds the fiction in a specific historical moment. It sets up our expectations for the novel as a story set in reality, expectations which are then radically challenged as the **narrative** progresses, and the story is passed from Lockwood to Nelly Dean.

KEY INTERPRETATION **A05**

Q. D. Leavis argues that Brontë set her radical and modernistic novel in the past in order to highlight the social challenges of the nineteenth century. This combination of modernist **themes** and style together with an insistence on historical context is one of the most compelling and fruitful contradictions in the novel.

The critic Q. D. Leavis links the importance of time in the novel to its social context. She remarks in her essay 'A Fresh Approach to *Wuthering Heights*': 'The point about dating this novel as ending in 1801 (instead of its being contemporary with the Brontës' own lives) … is to fix its happenings at a time when the old rough farming culture based on a naturally patriarchal family life, was to be challenged, tamed and routed by social and cultural changes' (reprinted in Patsy Stoneman (ed.), *Wuthering Heights: Contemporary Critical Essays*, 1993, p. 31).

In other words, by setting the story very clearly in the past, Brontë could demonstrate the point at which a whole way of life was to change, with the traditional values of the farming lifestyle challenged by ideas about progress, culture and civilisation.

VOLUME I, CHAPTER II

Summary

- Lockwood repeats his visit to the Heights and meets Hareton and Cathy Heathcliff.
- Lockwood mistakes a heap of dead rabbits for a cushion full of cats, revealing him as an unreliable observer, who sees only what he expects to see.
- He also antagonises Hareton by trying to guess at the family relationships, and in the end Heathcliff is obliged to explain that both his wife and his son are dead and that Cathy is his daughter-in-law.
- Because of a blizzard, Lockwood is forced to spend the night as a guest at the Heights.

Analysis

Lockwood the outsider

This chapter clearly conveys the structural and social differences between Lockwood's expectations and the conventions he comes into contact with in Yorkshire. His desire to dine at five, for example, reflects a non-labouring lifestyle. Through the character of Joseph, Brontë provides a convincing rendition of Yorkshire **dialect**, which again serves to position Lockwood as an outsider, unable to comprehend the ordinary **discourse** of the region. He is equipped with only his conventional notions of the world, and his pitiful misreading of the domestic situation stands as a warning against the assumption that a conventional understanding, or what seems like common sense, will be a reliable guide in this novel.

Key quotation: External descriptions   **A01**

Brontë uses external descriptions in this chapter to indicate Lockwood's internal state: 'A sorrowful sight I saw; dark night coming down prematurely, and sky and hills mingled into one bitter whirl of wind and suffocating snow. "I don't think it possible for me to get home now, without a guide"' (p. 14). This oppressive description, in which Lockwood uses the words 'sorrowful' and 'suffocating', reveals that he feels himself to be at the mercy of potentially threatening conditions, and cannot see his way to what is familiar territory.

A04 **KEY CONNECTION**

Note another reference to Shakespeare on page 17 – *King Lear*, Act II, Scene 4, lines 279–82. This reference to *King Lear* primarily serves to confirm Lockwood as educated (but not discerning). It might also be read as indicative of the themes of madness and rationality, inheritance and family power struggles, which are integral to this novel.

VOLUME I, CHAPTER III

Summary

- Zillah, the housekeeper at Wuthering Heights, shows Lockwood to a room at the top of the house which, she confides, is both secret and forbidden.

- The room is covered with the name 'Catherine' in different forms: Catherine Earnshaw, Catherine Linton, Catherine Heathcliff.

- Lockwood has two dreams. In the first he listens to a sermon by Jabes Branderham; in the second he sees the ghost of Catherine and rubs her wrist against the window pane, drawing blood.

- Lockwood cries out to the ghost, waking Heathcliff and causing him great distress.

- The next morning Heathcliff guides Lockwood back to the Grange, where he feels disorientated and 'feeble as a kitten' (p. 32).

Analysis

Dreams

This is a chapter which has received much critical attention. Containing Lockwood's two dreams, it clearly lends itself to a **psychoanalytic** reading, a reading which treats the novel itself like a dream, a fiction of the mind, which must be interpreted before its meaning can be clearly understood. As Philip K. Wion points out in his psychoanalytic reading of the novel ('The Absent Mother in Emily Brontë's *Wuthering Heights*', 1985), dreams and hallucinations are forms of seeing in which the boundaries between the self and the world are broken down, since in dreams the dreamer is often both an observer and a participant. The names inscribed upon the windowsill can be linked to the same idea, as they show Catherine's awareness of the conflicting elements of her own identity. The order they appear in marks her journey from child – Catherine Earnshaw; through her passionate years with Heathcliff – Catherine Heathcliff; to adulthood and marriage – Catherine Linton.

Dreams in this novel are both visionary, in that they help us to see beyond actual events, and mysterious. They are treated with respect and fear, for they show us an unpredictable and disturbing world. For Brontë, dreams offered a way of representing things which were way beyond the limits of literary decorum for the nineteenth-century novel. Almost all the dreams in this novel deal with taboo subjects: death, religion, love versus passion, and therefore probably helped to prompt the puzzled and outraged reviews that the novel received upon first publication.

Repetition and mirroring

Frank Kermode (1975) reads the repetitions of Catherine's names as evidence of the very isolated nature of the society, and also as essential to the structure of the story:

> you see the point of the order of the scribbled names, as Lockwood gives them: Catherine Earnshaw, Catherine Heathcliff, Catherine Linton. Read from left to right they recapitulate the late Catherine Earnshaw's story; read from right to left, the story of her daughter, Catherine Linton. The names Catherine and Earnshaw begin and end the narrative … this is an account of the movement of the book: away from Earnshaw and back, like the movement of the house itself. And all the movements must be through Heathcliff. (p. 139)

PROGRESS BOOSTER **A02**

Take note of key points you can analyse for AO2. The description of Lockwood as a kitten serves to identify him as similar to Edgar, who is described as a cat in Chapter VIII. Their similarities extend to their refined and fastidious natures, their education and their social status. It might also cause us to reflect on their capacity to form real relationships.

A **structuralist** reading of the chapter would focus upon the complex, interlocking structure of this text: what has been called its 'Chinese box' structure by C. P. Sanger ('The Structure of "Wuthering Heights"', 1926). Mirroring the text-within-a-text structure of the novel, the bedroom to which Lockwood is shown contains within it a cleverly designed panelled structure which serves as both bed and little closet. We have the bedroom within the bedroom, the texts within the text which are themselves **palimpsests**, written over with Catherine's diary entries; the dreams, which contain sleepiness within sleeping, texts within texts again, and secrets within secrets.

Progress booster: *Wuthering Heights* as parable

J. Hillis Miller's influential **deconstructive** reading of the chapter (*Fiction and Repetition*, 1982) discusses the palimpsestic nature of the texts, in which each text can be seen as a commentary upon a previous one. His reading follows this path: Catherine's diary is described by Lockwood as a commentary, written in the margins of Branderham's sermon. That sermon is itself a commentary upon a text of the New Testament in which Jesus enjoins his followers to forgive seventy times seven. The first of the seventy-first is therefore to be understood as the unpardonable sin. The story from the Bible is Jesus's interpretation of the nature of forgiveness, and includes a reading of several phrases from the Old Testament. Jesus's interpretation is characteristically accompanied by a **parable** (a story which explains or illustrates an abstract concept).

Wuthering Heights can be read as a parable, then, in that it is Lockwood's **narration** of a story which is adjacent to or in the margins of the mysterious events which he is trying to understand. Miller's reading focuses attention on the role of margins in this novel; he comments upon the difficulty of identifying the exact beginning of the novel, prefaced as it is by so many introductions. Lockwood's dreams can be seen as an example of precisely this difficulty of locating an exact beginning or meaning.

A03

A01 **PROGRESS BOOSTER**

There are many layers and repetitions in this novel, not only in the names of characters but in the overlaps between Volumes I and II. Examiners will be impressed if you use the literary term palimpsest to describe the different layers of meaning.

A05 **KEY INTERPRETATION**

In *Emily Brontë: Wuthering Heights* (Analysing Texts series, 1999), Nicholas Marsh provides an interesting analysis of whether Brontë uses ghosts and the supernatural in a conventionally **Gothic** sense and argues that her treatment invites comparisons with much later writers such as E. M. Forster and James Joyce. In this way, Brontë's use of the surreal can be seen to be ahead of her time.

Revision task 1: Repetition

A02

Write about repetition in *Wuthering Heights* in terms of the characters, plot events and images. Focus on:

- Names and characters
- Abduction/imprisonment
- Imagery

VOLUME I, CHAPTER IV

Summary

- While recovering from his trip to the Heights, Lockwood asks his housekeeper, Nelly Dean, to tell him the story of the inhabitants of Wuthering Heights.
- We learn that Cathy Heathcliff is the last of the Lintons, just as Hareton is the last of the Earnshaws.
- Nelly hints that Heathcliff has cheated Hareton out of his rightful inheritance.
- Nelly Dean takes over the **narration** at this point and we learn something of Heathcliff's history: how he was rescued from the port of Liverpool by Mr Earnshaw, his growing friendship with Catherine and his feud with her brother Hindley.
- Two years later Mrs Earnshaw dies and the children all fall ill with the measles. Heathcliff endears himself to Nelly as he does not complain, unlike Hindley and Catherine.
- The chapter closes with the incident of the two colts. Heathcliff takes the best and, when his falls lame, takes Hindley's.

Analysis

Heathcliff's arrival

From the moment he arrives, Heathcliff occupies a conflicting and contradictory position in the household, and in the story. He is both a ghostly substitute for a dead elder son and 'A wicked boy' (Vol. I, Ch. VI, p. 50) 'possessed of something diabolical' (Vol. I, Ch. VIII, p. 66). He is also quite beyond the formal societal constraints of the family and the Church, having but one name that serves him for both purposes.

Hindley's behaviour towards Heathcliff is brutish and violent. Heathcliff, once he gets his way, is self-contained and apparently unvindictive, though tantalisingly Nelly confides that in this assessment she was 'deceived, completely' (p. 40). Read in conjunction with the qualities he shows in illness, Heathcliff's attitude here can be seen as revealing of his unwavering ambition. He does not waste emotional energy, and he is oblivious to the emotional life of others.

KEY INTERPRETATION **A05**

It can be argued that Heathcliff's stoicism and patience in illness, which here are the qualities that endear him to Nelly, are precisely the qualities that he draws on later as he exacts his revenge on those around him. It is worth considering the extent to which the characters' strengths in *Wuthering Heights* also turn out to be precisely those things which provide the conditions for their downfall.

Study focus: Reading Heathcliff

The arrival of Heathcliff at the Heights has been the focus of much critical attention. In *The Madwoman in the Attic: The Woman Writer and the Nineteenth-Century Literary Imagination* (1979), Sandra Gilbert and Susan Gubar read this arrival in terms of gender roles, paying attention to the whip as a symbol of masculinity, which Catherine has requested and which is lost only to be replaced by Heathcliff.

In *Myths of Power: A Marxist Study of the Brontës* (1992), a **Marxist reading** of the novel, Terry Eagleton sees Heathcliff's presence at the Heights as both radical and random. Because Heathcliff's origins are so obscure, and because his family relationships place him outside the conventional social structure of the family, he can be be loved or hated for himself. His lack of social status or clear social role, coupled with Mr Earnshaw's favouritism, disrupts any certainty about rightful inheritance, causing Hindley to feel, rightly, threatened, and Catherine, equally rightly, strengthened.

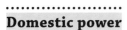

A new voice

The most significant aspect of this chapter is the change of narrator from Lockwood, whom we have come to see as unreliable, to Nelly Dean, who has the advantage of having lived with the main protagonists and who is thus able to explain their characters to Lockwood.

This doubling of narrator reminds us, as J. Hillis Miller points out, not to be too overconfident as readers. The switch from Lockwood to Nelly is immediately unsettling and removes our certainty that the narrator's voice is neutral or trustworthy. This device of an external masculine **narrative** framing and giving legitimacy to an internal feminine narrative was also used by Anne Brontë in *The Tenant of Wildfell Hall*. It can be seen in relation to Emily Brontë's use of the masculine-sounding **pseudonym** 'Ellis Bell' to legitimate her own novel.

Domestic power

When Nelly Dean takes up the story we are presented with a narrative whose subject and interest consist entirely of domestic action and adventure. The structure of power is an important **theme** for Brontë, and she treats it in a very complex way, revealing its contradictory yet never confused relationships. The prevailing wisdom about power in the nineteenth century was that men had it and women didn't. If women had any power at all, it was confined to the home. Brontë's characters, however, disrupt these ideas about power, who it belongs to and how they use it. While she is clearly aware of and understands the impact of property laws upon women's wealth and influence, Brontë suggests that we should not underestimate the domestic power that women are sometimes able to wield. At the end of the novel it is her female characters who have the upper hand: Cathy, bathed in glowing moonlight and the warmth from the fire, is teaching a willingly submissive Hareton his letters; similarly, Nelly is able to silence Joseph, and expertly manages the financial affairs of both properties.

A05 **KEY INTERPRETATION**

Nelly's description of the family tree curiously identifies Hareton as 'the late Mrs Linton's nephew' (p. 34) rather than the late Mr Earnshaw's son which subtly locates him in the house on which his name does not appear (Thrushcross Grange). This, it could be argued, prefigures the resolution of the novel.

Study focus: Power politics **A03**

To get the best grades at AS and A Level you need to show an excellent understanding of the contexts that lie behind the text. The relationship between the different kinds of power is elegantly exemplified in the relationship between the two narrators. Lockwood, although he is woefully incapable of reading the **discourse** of his new environment and utterly incompetent at understanding the writing on the sill, is nevertheless able as a man, and as Heathcliff's tenant, to prevail upon Nelly Dean to sit and tell him stories way beyond her working hours. Nelly, on the other hand, reader of all the books in the library and recipient of important letters, controls a great deal of the action of the novel through her choices about what to do with such privileged information.

Key quotation: 'from the devil' **A01**

The link that Brontë makes, through Nelly, between Heathcliff and the devil adds a **Gothic** element to the novel: 'you must e'en take [Heathcliff] as a gift of God; though it's as dark almost as if it came from the devil' (p. 36). From these first words Heathcliff is associated with the idea of a battle between heaven and hell. There is a sense of foreboding about Heathcliff's arrival – note how Mr Earnshaw's words can be read as a warning that the child must be treated with respect.

VOLUME I, CHAPTER V

Summary

- Nelly Dean recounts how the family relationships develop in divisive ways as Mr Earnshaw's health fails.
- Hindley continues to bully Heathcliff and humiliate him. On the advice of the curate who is offering the family private tuition, Hindley is eventually sent away to college, despite his father's doubts about its benefits.
- We are given our first sustained description of Catherine.
- Mr Earnshaw dies quietly one October evening. Both Catherine and Heathcliff are utterly distraught, and comfort each other.

Analysis

Contradictions and spirituality

The focus of this chapter is Catherine's relationships with her father and Heathcliff, of whom, Nelly suggests, Catherine is much too fond. However, the description of Catherine as deliberately infuriating and rebellious, and indeed of Heathcliff as some sort of devilish progeny, is counterbalanced by their response to her father's death, which Nelly describes as both anguished and innocent. Contradiction is seen to be an integral part of the way in which people relate to each other. It is this acknowledgement of internal contradiction that has led critics to see the novel as morally ambivalent. It is also worth noting that at this early point in the novel Brontë is already pitting an unmediated spiritual belief against the stern religious dogma of Joseph. When Catherine and Heathcliff comfort each other at Mr Earnshaw's death, Nelly Dean comments: 'no parson in the world ever pictured Heaven so beautifully as they did, in their innocent talk' (p. 44).

KEY CONNECTION A04

Emily Brontë often refers to the comfort to be gained from the idea of an afterlife in heaven. See, for example, a Gondal poem dated 1843, 'M.G. For the U.S. (Unique Society),' "T'was yesterday, at early dawn', in Emily Brontë, *A Peculiar Music* (ed. Naomi Lewis, Bodley Head, 1971), p. 51. It is worth considering to what extent she portrays heaven as a comfort in *Wuthering Heights*.

The impact of Heathcliff

As Mr Earnshaw's health begins to fail, his favouritism of Heathcliff becomes even more pronounced. Hindley continues to scorn Heathcliff, which enrages his weakening father. Nelly's hope that Hindley's removal would restore some peace to the household is undermined by a crucial unspoken acknowledgement. It seems that the source of the tension is Heathcliff: 'It hurt me to think the master should be made uncomfortable by his own good deed' (p. 41).

Religion and propriety

Brontë devotes very little physical description to Joseph. Almost all we know of him comes through his dialogue, which is often anchored in both biblical references and superstition. In contrast Catherine's liveliness extends to all those around her, including the old servant: 'she was never so happy as when we were all scolding her at once, and she defying us with her bold, saucy look, and her ready words; turning Joseph's religious curses into ridicule' (p. 43). We could argue that this shows Catherine to be a selfish and unsympathetic character and an unlikely heroine – she has no respect for authority, neither for her father, her nurse, nor for Joseph's religious authority. On the other hand, Joseph's lack of compassion towards the children's display of unrestrained grief when Mr Earnshaw dies – 'Joseph asked what we could be thinking of to roar in that way over a saint in Heaven.' (p. 44) – conveys their willingness to live a life of passion rather than one filtered through the context of religious propriety.

A04 KEY CONNECTION

Juliet Barker's biography of the Brontës (1994, revised 2010) has some particularly insightful passages about death and how important it was in the poetry of Emily Brontë and the novels of both Emily and Anne.

Key quotation: Wayward Catherine

The first description of Catherine shows her as beautiful, lively and wayward, but with a good heart: 'A wild, wick slip she was – but, she had the bonniest eye, and the sweetest smile, and the lightest foot in the parish; and, after all, I believe she meant no harm' (p. 42).

Here, the 'wild, wick slip' demonstrates Catherine's vitality, full of life in contrast to her dying father, and in contrast to the expectations of genteel girlhood.

Study focus: Childhood

A04

The descriptions of Catherine show her as spontaneous and impulsive, which sets up our expectations of her character as a Romantic heroine later in the novel. The vision of childhood that Brontë portrays is one in which the children are full of the authority of their own natural vitality. The passage has been read as an example of the Romantic **theme** of the child in conflict with society. If we accept such a reading, it is noteworthy that Brontë permits Catherine the last word: 'Why cannot you always be a good man, father?' (p. 43).

A02 PROGRESS BOOSTER

Be prepared for challenging questions. You may be asked about the importance of childhood in this novel, or to choose two of the minor characters and discuss their relevance to the main themes of the novel.

VOLUME I, CHAPTER VI

Summary

- Following the death of his father, Hindley returns as the master of the Heights, with a wife, Frances, who is described as poor, ill and 'silly' (p. 45).
- As the new master, Hindley is able to vent all his old hatred of Heathcliff. He denies him an education, insists that he should labour out of doors and makes him live with the servants.
- Despite Hindley's endeavours, Catherine and Heathcliff remain inseparable and wild.
- We have our first introduction to Edgar and Isabella Linton, who live at the neighbouring house, Thrushcross Grange.
- Catherine is hurt on one of her escapades with Heathcliff, and is obliged to remain at Thrushcross Grange until she is considered well enough to return to the Heights.

Analysis

Nature versus culture

Critics have often focused upon the structural differences between Thrushcross Grange and Wuthering Heights. The splendid, cultivated and civilised atmosphere at the Grange is compared with the rough indiscipline of the Heights. Most famously, David Cecil (*Victorian Novelists: Essays in Revaluation*, 1935) has argued that the differences between the Heights and the Grange can be thought of as corresponding to a **metaphysical** opposition between storm and calm. And yet, as Gilbert and Gubar (*The Madwoman in the Attic: The Woman Writer and the Nineteenth-Century Literary Imagination*, 1979) point out, the violence which one might naturally associate with the Heights is no less present at the Grange. They argue that Catherine, for example, does not so much willingly enter the world of Thrushcross Grange, but rather is seized by it. Indeed, as Terry Eagleton (1992) points out, the more property one has, the more ferociously one needs to protect it (see **Violence at the Grange**, below).

In their reading of the novel in Chapter 8 of *The Madwoman in the Attic,* the **feminist critics** Sandra Gilbert and Susan Gubar see *Wuthering Heights* as a 'Bible of Hell' in that it is a novel which privileges the natural over the cultural, the freedom of anarchy over domestic life and repressed feelings. The domain of Wuthering Heights is certainly anarchic judged by conventional standards. Indeed, in Chapter II we are encouraged by Lockwood to read it as hellish with his remarks upon the 'dismal spiritual atmosphere' (Vol. I, Ch. II, p. 14) and Heathcliff's 'almost diabolical' (Vol. I, Ch. II, p. 13) smile. But it can also be read as representing another challenge to convention in that it is an ungovernable social space, in other words one without authority. As such, it is a space in which both Catherine and Heathcliff can exercise power. In almost any other environment in the nineteenth century this power would be denied to them, she being female and he being illegitimate.

Violence at the Grange

Violence characterises life at Wuthering Heights, where the children are often beaten, in apparent contrast to the 'petted' (p. 48) lives of the children at Thrushcross Grange. So it is worth paying attention to the fact that Thrushcross Grange is the site of the first real act of aggression in either of the two houses. As Catherine and Heathcliff peep in through the windows of the Grange, they are noticed and set upon by guard dogs and Catherine is caught by the ankle and savaged. Thus she is unable to return to the Heights with Heathcliff.

KEY CONTEXT A03

Catherine's courage in this chapter is reminiscent of Emily Brontë's own fearlessness in the face of great pain. In one incident, Emily used a red-hot iron to cauterise a wound she sustained from a ferocious dog.

KEY CONTEXT A03

This depiction of domestic violence is entirely in conflict with the conventional Victorian notion of the home as the ideal refuge from the harshness of the outside world.

Captured, in fairy-tale manner, by the 'civilised' world of Thrushcross Grange, Catherine yields to what she understands to be her destiny, even as she sees that this life is quite opposite to her character. Later, anguished and despairing, she resists her life with Edgar Linton and finds her only way out of it by death. Literally she 'catches her death' by throwing open the window in Chapter XII. This act of opening the window can be read as rupturing the fortifications of the civilised life to let in the fresh air of the natural, an act of such **symbolic** violence that it can only result in death.

Study focus: A mirror image

A02

Heathcliff admires the comparative luxury of the Grange and acknowledges its beauty. He even compares it to a kind of heaven, but he remains entirely devoted to the freedom of his life with Catherine, and cannot comprehend the selfishness of the spoiled children: 'When would you catch me wishing to have what Catherine wanted?' (p. 48).

This question is **rhetorical**. What Heathcliff cannot imagine is quarrelling with Catherine over something she wants, since their needs and desires are exactly matched. What appalls him are the opposing, individual, selfish needs of the Linton children. The image of the two civilised children inside the beautiful room, and the two wild children outside, both pairs a boy and girl of similar ages, can be read as though the glass of the window is a kind of mirror. However, this is a mirror which reflects opposition, desire and otherness. It has thus provided rich material for both **structuralist** and **psychoanalytic** readings.

Heathcliff's language

This chapter gives the child Heathcliff his first major speech, and it is worth noting how his language differs from that of the other characters. He is expressive and emotional, and this encourages us to identify with his unmediated, unguarded response. His speech is more literary than Nelly's and less artificial than Lockwood's. He tends to speak in extreme and vibrant terms. Expressing his scorn for Edgar Linton's cowardice and weak politeness, he says:

> I'd not exchange, for a thousand lives, my condition here, for Edgar Linton's at Thrushcross Grange – not if I might have the privilege of flinging Joseph off the highest gable, and painting the house-front with Hindley's blood! (p. 49)

Note that in aligning ourselves with Heathcliff as the vital and wronged party here we are already accepting and endorsing the violence that is to characterise his behaviour as the novel progresses. Heathcliff's threat to paint the house with Hindley's blood and fling Joseph off the gable top is an empty one at this point, but it nevertheless presages what is to come. It can also be read as representing a real desire to topple conventional religious authority in favour of a more 'natural' spirituality and to sever the authority of Hindley's bloodline, making Wuthering Heights his own.

A03 **KEY INTERPRETATION**

As Alexander and Smith note in *The Oxford Companion to the Brontës* (2003), the 'family knew the works of Shakespeare almost as well as they did the Bible'. The connection between blood and revenge is central to both this novel and *Macbeth*.

VOLUME I, CHAPTER VII

Summary

- Catherine returns from her five-week stay at Thrushcross Grange, transformed into a lady.
- Heathcliff has been systematically degraded by Hindley during this time.
- The Linton children have been invited to Wuthering Heights the next day in order to thank them for nursing Catherine.
- Heathcliff begs Nelly to make him presentable, but Hindley and Edgar Linton both try to humiliate Heathcliff, who retaliates violently.
- Heathcliff is dismissed and Catherine, apparently unfeelingly, continues to have tea with her new friends.
- Eventually she creeps away from the tea party to be with Heathcliff, and Heathcliff plots his revenge on Hindley.
- The end of this chapter reminds us that this is a story being related to Lockwood by Nelly Dean.

Analysis

Two different worlds

This chapter is the first to demonstrate explicitly the differences between the two houses, Thrushcross Grange and Wuthering Heights – differences that represent the central oppositions of the novel. Catherine stays at Thrushcross Grange for five weeks until she is deemed healthy, both in body and in manners. She returns to the Heights a very 'dignified person' (p. 53), dressed in fine clothes and quite transformed from the person she has been. We can see that Thrushcross Grange therefore **symbolises** civilisation and status. Heathcliff, by contrast, is forbiddingly unkempt, but Catherine's love of him is undiminished and she embraces him immediately.

Boundaries and barriers

The concept of boundaries and barriers is key to this chapter. Just as the window separated the Wuthering Heights children from the Lintons in the last chapter, here too a material object separates Catherine from Heathcliff. The fine dress she wears to return to the Heights represents a very real boundary between the old friends: it must be sacrificed (smudged, crumpled) if the two of them are to be as close as they were before. It is valuable simultaneously for economic reasons (its cost), for social ones (the respect it earns Catherine), and because of its artificial beauty. These same categories will consistently come between Catherine and Heathcliff: he is right to recognise the dress and what it represents as a threat to his happiness. The dress thus signifies the artifice of civilisation which Catherine must put on and which will alienate her from Heathcliff, with devastating consequences.

KEY INTERPRETATION **A03**

As Ruth Robbins clarifies in *Literary Feminisms* (2000): 'Thrushcross Grange, across the moor, home of the Linton family, represents the standards of patriarchal culture which will be triumphant at the end of the story, but which the novel itself, through its sympathies for Cathy and Heathcliff, implicitly attacks' (p. 92).

KEY INTERPRETATION **A05**

The bed to which Heathcliff retires hurt is precisely the bed which had housed Lockwood's disturbing dreams in the third chapter. Here, too, its panels and windows operate to form a series of boundaries behind which secrets can be concealed.

Nelly and Lockwood

Nelly Dean interrupts her **narrative** to focus upon Lockwood, who requires her to continue her story even though it is late in the day. Lockwood comments on the class and type of people he has encountered in the region, and Nelly calls his hasty judgements and patronising attitude to our attention by remarking that he 'could not open a book in this library that [she had] not looked into' (p. 63). Lockwood's failure to read Nelly Dean in any terms other than the conventions of class is further reinforced by his insensitivity to Nelly's hours of sleep and work. She characteristically deflates his pompous speech on the type of people native to the region by drawing attention to both her level of formal education and the lessons learned from the demanding aspects of her life. A **feminist reading** of the novel would consider how Brontë emphasises the power of female **discourse** with Nelly's account here. Lockwood's inability to contemplate the broader picture is perceived by both Nelly and the reader to be a failure of intellect as much as of experience.

A05 KEY INTERPRETATION

Michael Macovski's essay 'Voicing a Silent History: *Wuthering Heights* as Dialogic Text' (1987; reprinted in Patsy Stoneman (ed.), *Wuthering Heights: Contemporary Critical Essays*, 1993) offers an intriguing reading of the novel as a series of stories.

Religion and freedom

This chapter once again offers an interestingly nuanced view of religion. Joseph's surly, isolated religion which sees him retiring in 'private prayer' is pitted against Nelly's conventionally celebratory religion 'singing carols' (p. 55), and then further contrasted with the free-spirited life of the children as Heathcliff, waiting until the rest of the family have departed for church, goes out onto the moors which returns him 'to a better spirit' (p. 56) and makes him determined to be good.

A03

Study focus: Emily Brontë and religion

Brontë's views on religion were highly unorthodox in Victorian society, and would have been very radical ideas to her readership. They might seem particularly unorthodox for the daughter of a parson but, in fact, they are indicative of the fact that her father believed in a great many freedoms for his children, not least of which was intellectual freedom. Katherine Frank remarks on Emily Brontë's 'peculiar faith' in her book *Emily Brontë: A Chainless Soul* (1990). She draws on examples from Emily Brontë's poetry to show that Emily was not a Christian in the conventional sense of the term. Make sure you can write about the importance of religion, and different forms of spirituality, in the novel.

A03

Revision task 2: Religion

Write about the role of religion in the novel and the way in which Emily Brontë"s own beliefs form a key context for the novel. Focus on:

● The dream of the Branderham sermon

● The character of Joseph: his puritanical approach

● Catherine and Heathcliff

● Edgar Linton's view of religion and his behaviour towards Isabella and Catherine

● Nelly Dean's view of religion

Lockwood and love

At the end of the chapter Lockwood remarks to Nelly Dean: 'I could fancy a love for life here almost possible; and I was a fixed unbeliever in any love' (p. 62). This is a revealing speech from Lockwood and shows him yet again in a negative light. For Brontë, love is the supreme redeemer but Lockwood describes himself as an 'unbeliever'. It reminds us that this is a story within a story, being told by people who have no understanding of each other. It also shows that Lockwood has a limited grasp of the fierce passions of the central characters.

Key quotation: Heathcliff's revenge **A01**

On page 61, Heathcliff tells Nelly that he is 'trying to settle how I shall pay Hindley back. I don't care how long I wait, if I can only do it, at last. I hope he will not die before I do!' When Nelly urges the importance of forgiveness and that it is 'for God to punish wicked people', Heathcliff is defiant:

> 'No, God won't have the satisfaction that I shall,' he returned. 'I only wish I knew the best way! Let me alone, and I'll plan it out: while I'm thinking of that, I don't feel pain.' (p. 61)

This emphasis on revenge blocking out physical pain is the first intimation of Heathcliff's character that sets him on the tragic journey from abandoned orphan to loveless tyrant.

It links Heathcliff's words to the wider **theme** of good and evil and shows that Heathcliff lives outside religious faith and moral laws.

Revision task 3: Class and empathy **A03**

Write about the importance of class mobility and class divisions to the structure of *Wuthering Heights*. Focus on:

- Lockwood and his relationships
- The different experiences for Catherine at Thrushcross Grange and Wuthering Heights
- Cathy and her relationships with the other characters
- Heathcliff's transformation

VOLUME I, CHAPTER VIII

Summary

- In June 1778, Hindley's son Hareton is born.
- Frances Earnshaw dies of consumption and Hindley descends even further into recklessness. Nelly Dean returns to Wuthering Heights to act as nursemaid to the baby.
- The relationship between Catherine and Edgar develops, and the tension between Edgar and Heathcliff intensifies. Catherine is torn between them.
- Catherine displays violent behaviour, pinching Nelly and boxing Edgar's ears.

Analysis

Catherine's choice

This chapter explicitly details the central conflict of the novel: the choice that Catherine has to make between Heathcliff and Edgar Linton. The choice is pivotal to all the events in the novel. It has been variously seen as a choice between passion and social status, authenticity and bad faith, sex and sublimation, risk and security, nature and culture, spirituality and economics. However it is framed, the choice is almost always seen as being between two incompatible ways of life. Catherine's attempts throughout the novel to reconcile the two result in her death, suggesting that they really are fatally opposed realities.

'A naughty spirit'

The chapter also demonstrates Catherine's unruly temper. She transgresses the boundaries of good behaviour in increasing levels of violence. Edgar is shocked at Catherine's assault first on Nelly and then himself.

Catherine's violence can also be seen as a **metaphor** for her attempts to **transcend** her internal conflicts, and we can argue that it anticipates the unquietness of her ghost. Nelly says of Edgar that he 'wanted spirit in general' (p. 67), while Catherine has a 'naughty spirit' (p. 71). It is possible to read this both literally and in the context of the supernatural in this novel, for in the end Catherine's spirit transcends death and refuses to be quiet.

Progress booster: Linking form and theme (A01)

In her book *The English Novel: Form and Function* (1961), Dorothy Van Ghent draws our attention to the ways in which form supports the thematic structure of the novel. She observes that the aim to cross physical boundaries represents a wish to transcend psychological barriers and a desire to unite the two incompatible kinds of reality. There are several ways in which the form does this. The dual **narration** which **'frames'** the story in different ways points to the theme of boundaries and transgression. The fact that the narration is contradictory and sometimes confusing suggests that truth is not tidily contained in what we perceive as 'natural' or 'normal', but that it has to be striven for. Van Ghent puts forward an interesting argument that by the end of the novel Heathcliff's daughter-in-law, Cathy succeeds in achieving the domestic romance.

Van Ghent's thesis has been immensely influential. Searching for consistent images is now a standard method of reading a text and is one you can try yourself.

A03 KEY CONTEXT

Hindley's wife, Frances, exhibits the symptoms of tuberculosis or consumption, the disease which was to claim the lives of both Emily and Anne Brontë within six months of each other in 1848–9.

A01 PROGRESS BOOSTER

You can improve your grade by drawing parallels between a character's external behaviour and their internal state. Catherine's reluctance for Heathcliff and Edgar to meet stems from the feeling that their differences only highlight her own internal conflicts.

KEY INTERPRETATION **A05**

Brontë's use of nature as a **pathetic fallacy**, and her descriptions of nature affecting the emotional states of her characters owes much to the aesthetic idea of the **sublime** as proposed by Edmund Burke in his essay, 'A Philosophical Enquiry into the Origins of Our Ideas of the Sublime and the Beautiful' (1757). Burke describes the sublime as provoking feelings of terror and pleasure. The summer storm that accompanies Heathcliff's rage and despair when he overhears Catherine telling Nelly it would degrade her to marry him, prompts feelings of sublime terror in Nelly and Joseph.

KEY INTERPRETATION **A05**

Pauline Nester suggests a different view of love in her introduction to the 1995 Penguin edition of the novel: 'while the novel may seem to hold out the promise of such satisfaction on this level, in a more complex and more interesting way it actually investigates rather than exemplifies the romantic cliché of perfect love' (p. x). These are useful points to consider when forming an argument about whether this novel is primarily a love story.

VOLUME I, CHAPTER IX

Summary

- Heathcliff and Hindley's relationship deteriorates even further. Hindley is abusive and violent to everyone, threatens Nelly with a carving knife and shows no affection for his infant son.
- Catherine makes her choice between Edgar and Heathcliff and chooses Edgar. There is a long discussion between Catherine and Nelly Dean on the nature of love. Catherine makes it clear that she has chosen to marry Edgar for his looks, his wealth and his position. She says it would 'degrade' (p. 81) her to marry Heathcliff, at which Heathcliff, who has been listening unobserved, disappears.
- Catherine is distraught and goes to search for him on the moors, as a consequence of which she catches a fever and goes once more to recuperate at the Grange.
- Three years later, when Edgar is master of the Grange, he marries Catherine. Heathcliff is absent all this time.
- Nelly reluctantly leaves Hareton and goes with Catherine to live at the Grange.

Analysis

Love and marriage

On one level this novel can be read as the supreme celebration of a love story, describing a love which defies authority, social convention, even death. Catherine and Heathcliff's love is famously deferred, never consummated and never brought down to the level of trivial day-to-day matters. Theirs is a love which is idealised and magnified, and, in positing such a relationship, the novel both recognises and explicitly appeals to the desire for perfect love.

The central **theme** of the novel is revealed here as being about the contradictory experiences of love and marriage: Catherine agonises about the practical choice she must make in choosing her future. She recognises that she must choose Edgar, for the implications this has for her and her children's lives; but she refuses to accept that this means forgoing Heathcliff and a life of passion. Catherine's conflict is not just a matter of personal preference. As a nineteenth-century woman, the consequences for her well-being and that of any children she might have are very starkly affected by the choices she makes. Brontë is acutely aware of the real social implications of marriage for a woman.

Catherine describes her thoughts on love through a dream she has had about being unfit to enter heaven (pp. 80–1). **Psychoanalytic critics** have focused their attention on the dreams in this novel and the ways in which desire is diverted into other, destructive, channels. Other critics, such as **Marxist** and **feminist critics**, have read Catherine's choice between Edgar and Heathcliff in terms of its political implications.

Catherine puts forward her thoughts on marriage as 'a secret' which is making her 'very unhappy' (p. 77). She reveals that she has agreed to marry Edgar Linton for reasons which are, according to Nelly Dean, at best indifferent (because he loves her) and at worst immoral (because they are self-seeking): 'he will be rich, and I shall like to be the greatest woman of the neighbourhood, and I shall be proud of having such a husband' (p. 78).

Study focus: A turning point

A02

Catherine's declaration of love for Heathcliff comes at precisely the moment when she has chosen to marry Edgar, and at the point at which Heathcliff disappears from their lives. It is therefore possible to read this as evidence of how in the novel the consummation of passion is endlessly put off in favour of social convention and restraint. Catherine's uncontrolled love for Heathcliff, which causes her to stay outdoors until she catches the chill which proves deadly to Mr and Mrs Linton, seems incompatible with civilised life, so much so that we could even argue that it kills it.

We can see Catherine's vow that anyone who tried to keep her and Heathcliff separate would 'meet the fate of Milo' (p. 82) as a sign that she sees herself trapped between the two worlds.

A03 KEY CONTEXT

Milo was a Greek athlete who attempted to tear an oak in two, but found himself trapped when the cleft closed over his hands. This reference to Catherine being as trapped as Milo in her conflict is reiterated at the end of the first volume when Heathcliff declares: 'And that insipid, paltry creature attending her from *duty* and *humanity*! From *pity* and *charity*! He might as well plant an oak in a flower-pot, and expect it to thrive, as imagine he can restore her to vigour in the soil of his shallow cares!' (Vol. I, Ch. XIV, p. 152).

Key quotation: Dreams

A01

Catherine asks Nelly if she ever has strange dreams and then describes the effect of her own dreams:

> 'I've dreamt in my life dreams that have stayed with me ever after, and changed my ideas; they've gone through and through me, like wine through water, and altered the colour of my mind' (p. 80).

Catherine's earlier speech in Volume I, Chapter IV, about the power of dreams to change lives and to affect reality directly shows that dreams and dreaming is a recurring theme in the novel. For further analysis see **Extract Analysis: Volume 1, Chapter IX**.

EXTRACT ANALYSIS

Volume I, Chapter IX, pp. 79–81

From 'All seems smooth and easy – where is the obstacle?' to 'as different as a moonbeam from lightning or frost from fire.'

Following the violent incident between Hindley, Heathcliff and Hareton, there comes Catherine's account of Edgar's proposal and her response. She divulges this first in the form of a secret and then of a dream. Nelly fiercely resists the knowledge: '"I won't hear it, I won't hear it!" [...] I was superstitious about dreams then, and am still' (p. 80). The centrality of dreams in this novel permits Brontë to tackle subjects in ways which she simply could not have attempted had she stuck to the limitations of what Julia Swindells (*Victorian Writing and Working Women*, 1985) has called the literary professionalism of the 'Gentleman's Club' in the nineteenth century. Dreams enable Brontë to present ideas about love, religion and identity which would have been thoroughly shocking to the Victorian readership. The novel's violations and reinventions of identity, sexuality and religious taboo are as uncensored as in a dream: they are free from the restrictions of convention. Dreams do not insist upon one story, but often involve many overlapping stories. They often contain contradictions that may well be disturbing, but these contradictions are part of the very structure of dreaming.

Catherine's interpretation of her dream is key to our understanding of her perception of conventional marriage. It is perceived as a kind of paradise, a heaven on earth, but not one to which she feels she can belong:

> I was only going to say that heaven did not seem to be my home; and I broke my heart with weeping to come back to earth; and the angels were so angry that they flung me out, into the middle of the heath on the top of Wuthering Heights; where I woke sobbing for joy. (p. 81)

Notably, in this dream Catherine perceives her choices as moral choices, as choices between good and evil, heaven and hell, and she states that she cannot belong in the realm of heaven but must return to Wuthering Heights, where her joy is to be found.

KEY CONTEXT **A03**

The ballad that Nelly sings to Hareton expresses the widely held belief in folklore and folksong that a prematurely dead mother cannot rest in the grave but will return to suckle her baby or help her child when it is in need. It is thus prescient of what is to come.

KEY CONTEXT **A03**

Gentlemen's clubs were exclusive clubs that expanded greatly in the 1800s, in large part thanks to the Reform Acts of 1832, 1867 and 1885. As more men became entitled to vote, they felt that their status was elevated to that of 'gentlemen'. The clubs were characterised by their members' interests in literature, sport, politics or travel. Brontë's sensitivity to the political realities of women's lives is key to an understanding of the choices Catherine makes in this novel.

This dream references the central tension in the novel, between the Christian world of the Lintons, a world in which love is conceived of as Christian charity and social decorum, and the world of Heathcliff, a world of authentic love, which is passionate and unrestrained. But the heavenly world of the Lintons is perceived by Catherine to be a hollow world, a world that cannot be right:

> In whichever place the soul lives – in my soul and in my heart, I'm convinced I'm wrong! [...] I've no more business to marry Edgar Linton than I have to be in heaven; (pp. 80–1)

She is wrong to marry Edgar, because heaven is not a place in which her soul could ever be happy. Nelly endorses this when she says 'Because you are not fit to go there … All sinners would be miserable in heaven.' (p. 80). Later in the novel, Heathcliff insists that these heavenly sentiments of pity and charity would produce a living hell in the absence of real passion.

There is a contradiction, then, in the novel's treatment of the Christian virtue of love. On the one hand it shows Heathcliff as devilish and hardly human. On the other, it suggests that Christian love is self-serving and mean-spirited. In the whole novel, it is only Heathcliff who lays down his life for the love of another. Heathcliff's love is shown as **transcendent**, and deeper than the love of ordinary men.

Sigmund Freud's *The Interpretation of Dreams*, generally taken to be his major and most original work, can offer a different perspective on this passage. Freud investigates dreams, and the phenomenon of dreaming, as the products of a conflict between conscious and unconscious processes of thought. Freud reads the strange images and events experienced in dreams as coded **narratives** of the ways in which the unconscious mind is shaped by childhood events. According to his theory, the unconscious mind, repressed by the conscious mind in everyday life, finds expression in the form of dreaming. Applying Freud's theory to this passage, it is interesting to note that Catherine's dream retains its potency precisely because of its repression – she has physically to hold Nelly Dean down to make her listen to it. Furthermore, Catherine begins the account with a denial of it – 'This is nothing' (p. 81) – and a declaration of the conflict between her feelings for Edgar and for Heathcliff.

Catherine's desires, as expressed in her dream, are acknowledged to be immoral, making her unfit for heaven. Using Freudian terms, the dream provides a means of explaining a secret, illicit desire buried in her unconscious mind. This desire is revealed as a desire for the perverse and the unattainable. Because Edgar Linton is incorporated into the structures of allowable desire, he becomes less attractive, shifting attention back to Heathcliff. It seems that, for Brontë, true desire is not directed at an obtainable object, for this would allow the satisfaction of that desire. Instead, desire is most powerful when it is transgressive and when the satisfaction of it is impossible to achieve.

A03 **KEY CONNECTION**

In *The Interpretation of Dreams* (1953), Sigmund Freud offers a detailed investigation of the function of dreams, and the relationship between dreams and thoughts. A psychological interpetation of *Wuthering Heights* would focus on the role of dreams and hidden desires.

EXTRACT ANALYSIS

Volume I, Chapter IX, pp. 81–3

From 'I see no reason that he should not know, as well as you' to 'trouble me with no more secrets. I'll not promise to keep them.'

These pages contain the most powerfully expressed account of the nature of love in the whole novel, while also contributing to the development of some of the novel's central thematic oppositions: joy and redemption; belonging and exclusion; constancy and transience.

For many readers, the fascination and enduring appeal of *Wuthering Heights* lies in its evocation of romantic love, the state of being utterly absorbed in another person, which can be seen as a potent, nostalgic re-enactment of the oneness experienced by mother and child before the child acquires language. This oneness is elegantly expressed by Catherine:

> My great miseries in this world have been Heathcliff's miseries, and I watched and felt each from the beginning; my great thought in living is himself. If all else perished, and *he* remained, I should still continue to be; and, if all else remained, and he were annihilated, the Universe would turn to a mighty stranger. I should not seem a part of it. (p. 82)

The psychologist Jacques Lacan identifies an important phase of human development as being what he calls the 'mirror phase' of infancy, in which the self is defined not through language but through the reflecting gaze of somebody else (usually the mother) who is 'more myself than I am' (p. 81). Simply put, before they acquire language, children identify so powerfully with their mothers that they fail to see the difference between themselves and their mother. **Psychoanalytic readings** of *Wuthering Heights* have made much of this theory. Yet because the novel is, necessarily, bound in words, it can only use words to describe this pre-verbal state. This results in the passionate statement from Catherine, which is, strictly speaking, linguistic non-sense: 'I *am* Heathcliff' (p. 82).

The question of whether or not this story is the most perfect example of a love story is a controversial one. Central to our understanding of the story is how we respond to the question of love. Is it love that characterises the relationship between Catherine and Heathcliff or is it, more perplexingly, just passion? If it is love, then theirs is a love which leads them to identify so much with each other, and share their feelings so deeply, that the intense identification becomes fatal. If it is love, then it is a love which requires the absolute absence of the self. If it is love, then it is a love so beyond the conventions of romantic love that it becomes at the end an erotic obsession with death that is ultimately repellent.

The potency of the relationship between Catherine and Heathcliff brings to the novel its focus for examining the boundaries of identity. When Catherine declares to Nelly that she is Heathcliff, she offers a radical challenge to conventional notions of selfhood and individuality. Catherine's identification with Heathcliff in this passage utterly overwhelms her own individual personal identity.

This asks a profound philosophical question: what happens to identity when individuality collides with love, in whatever form: sexual, romantic or religious? For Catherine, this can be read as a stark choice about survival. Marriage to Heathcliff would not only exclude her from a traditional Christian version of heaven but would also threaten her ability to survive in an earthly, social context. As a daughter who could not expect to inherit any property, she rightly comments that her economic and social survival depends on marriage.

KEY INTERPRETATION **A05**

See Heather Glen's 'Critical Commentary' in her edition of *Wuthering Heights* (1988), pp. 360–1 for a good, non-technical discussion of some of these **themes**.

KEY INTERPRETATION **A03**

It can be argued that this dilemma lies at the heart of Catherine's choice: without Heathcliff she could not exist as herself, but without a legitimate social role and position, neither she nor Heathcliff could live at all.

Nelly Dean's role in this passage is also significant, for where Catherine's impassioned declarations of love, and marriage, are instinctive, Nelly provides the rationalist counterpart. She makes it clear that Catherine's reasons for marriage are bad ones, and crucially she points out that Catherine's wish to marry Edgar and maintain her relationship with Heathcliff is both impractical and unprincipled:

> and if *you* are his choice, he'll be the most unfortunate creature that ever was born! As soon as you become Mrs Linton, he loses friend, and love, and all! Have you considered how you'll bear the separation, and how he'll bear to be quite deserted in the world? (pp. 81–2)

Catherine agrees to marry Edgar Linton, not for love, but for social mobility. Linton will offer her security in ways that she perceives to be impossible for Heathcliff: 'if Heathcliff and I married, we should be beggars' (p. 82).

Further down the page, Catherine declares:

> My love for Linton is like the foliage in the woods. Time will change it, I'm well aware, as winter changes the trees – my love for Heathcliff resembles the eternal rocks beneath – a source of little visible delight, but necessary.

Catherine perceives her real, eternal, underlying life as being inextricably bound to Heathcliff. By contrast, her feelings for Edgar Linton are subject to change and are impermanent. Catherine perceives her love for Heathcliff to be unquestionable, a given fact. Like the earth or the sky, it is part of the fundamental texture of her life. It is worth noting that the contrasting images are both drawn from the real, natural world that Catherine perceives around her, and are therefore offered up as being authentically and inarguably true.

Through the character of Catherine in this passage, passionately committed to nature, but living in the midst of the culture that defines her, Brontë challenges the opposition of culture and nature, male and female, that were being fiercely debated in the period in which Brontë was writing. Nature was traditionally linked with the female and culture with the male realm, yet Catherine is presented here as an object of exchange within the social contract of marriage and therefore central to the perpetuation of the cultural as opposed to the natural world. Her role remains a fairly passive one – her choice is between two men, only one of whom can provide a secure future, and the idea of remaining unmarried as an independent woman is not even contemplated.

Yet the desire that characterises the love between Catherine and Heathcliff is likened to 'the eternal rocks' – beyond the realms of both masculine culture and nature in its traditionally feminine, tame form. It is described as having no need of words; it is beyond language. Situated between nature and culture, participating in both and owing an allegiance to neither, the characters of Catherine and Heathcliff can be read as a challenge to that established opposition.

A04 **KEY CONNECTION**

This passage recalls Shakespeare's sonnet 116 which claims love is an 'ever fixed marke' and 'Not Time's fool'.

VOLUME I, CHAPTER X

Summary

- Catherine Earnshaw is now married to Edgar Linton and lives in relative luxury and peace, indulged by Edgar and his sister Isabella.
- Heathcliff returns to the area, to Catherine's immense joy. Nelly remarks upon the transformation of Heathcliff into a tall, well-built, intelligent man.
- Heathcliff reveals that he is staying with Hindley Earnshaw at the Heights, which causes Nelly to be suspicious.
- Isabella develops an intense infatuation with Heathcliff, which he does not return. Nevertheless, he sees that he might use her feelings for him as a way to revenge himself upon Edgar.

Analysis

Heathcliff's energy

KEY INTERPRETATION **A05**

Ian Brinton's analysis of *Wuthering Heights* (Continuum, 2010) offers a sustained reading of the relationship between revenge and greed (pp. 60–8).

The return of Heathcliff to the text restores some of its sinister energy. It also seems to enliven Catherine and Isabella, taking them out of the atmosphere of Thrushcross Grange and onto the moors or up to the Heights. The return of Heathcliff also reinforces the truth of Catherine's insight in the previous chapter – 'If I were in heaven, Nelly, I should be extremely miserable' (Vol. I, Ch. IX, p. 80) – for her soul is the same as Heathcliff's, 'and Linton's is as different as a moonbeam from lightning, or frost from fire' (Vol. I, Ch. IX, p. 81). The energy of Heathcliff is a burning elemental energy which reinvigorates the **narrative** tension.

Love and revenge

Revenge might seem to be one of the main motivating factors in this novel, yet close analysis of Heathcliff's character shows that almost always revenge is secondary to his overriding love for Catherine. Everything that he does is about reuniting him with Catherine. However, Brontë is always alive to the financial realities of her characters, and another important element of Heathcliff's revenge has to do with avarice and property.

A02

Study focus: Animal imagery

Note the animal imagery that Brontë employs here. Towards the end of this chapter Catherine reiterates the association of Thrushcross Grange with heaven when she describes Isabella's eyes: 'They are dove's eyes – angel's' (p. 107). This, with its echo of an early description of Edgar as dove-like, prompts Heathcliff to consider the structures of inheritance, and thus form a plan for revenge. Heathcliff, a 'fierce, pitiless, wolfish man' (p. 103), who is described as a 'bird of bad omen' (p. 103) by Nelly, a 'knave' who laughs at any 'divil's jest' by Joseph (p. 104), and an 'evil beast' (p. 107) again by Nelly, is by his own admission 'ghoulish' (p. 106). All these descriptions are ranged against Isabella, who is described as a canary, a dove and an egg. However, Brontë is clear that these distinctions are not simple, as Isabella is also described as a tigress and a vixen (both p. 106), and it is Catherine who seeds the idea in Heathcliff's head about inheritance, when she announces: 'It lies in your own power to be Edgar's brother' (p. 105).

VOLUME I, CHAPTER XI

Summary

- Nelly returns on a whim to the Heights and is appalled to see how it has deteriorated.
- Hareton, previously her charge and joy, curses her though he is still barely more than five years old.
- Heathcliff calls at the Grange and makes overtures to Isabella, displeasing both Catherine and Edgar.
- Fierce arguments between Catherine, Edgar and Heathcliff induce Catherine to retire to her bed.

Analysis

Two households

Reminiscence marks the opening of this chapter, as Nelly Dean fondly remembers both her own childhood with Hindley and her affection for Hareton. Wuthering Heights again appears as the site of brutality and revenge. This is in marked contrast to the luxury and calm of the Grange. Heathcliff, it emerges, has set son against father and is inciting revolt in the already unhappy household. At the same time, Heathcliff's next visit to the Grange sees him capitalise upon Isabella's affection. This is an important chapter when considering whether or not Heathcliff is a truly vengeful character as we see his effect on both households.

Hot and cold

The relationship between Catherine and Edgar is once again considered in terms of extremes of temper and temperature – 'your veins are full of ice-water – but mine are boiling' (p. 117) – and Catherine retires to her bed claiming herself to be 'in danger of being seriously ill' (p. 116). Forced to choose between Edgar and Heathcliff, she threatens 'to break their hearts by breaking [her] own' (p. 116). Nelly treats Catherine's outburst as histrionics and fails to take her threatened illness seriously. Catherine departs to her room and refuses any nourishment for the next two days. Edgar retires to the library and tries to dissuade Isabella from her infatuation with Heathcliff, claiming that if she continues in it he will disown her. Who to love and the financial implications of that decision are revealed to be stark choices for women in the novel, as passion is contrasted with calm rationality and the promise of security.

Study focus: Heathcliff's torment (A02)

This is a key chapter for studying Heathcliff's character development. He has returned dominant and physically superior to the other characters, but his life is tormented. He accuses Catherine of treating him 'infernally' and of torturing him 'to death for [her] amusement' (p. 112). From now on there is scarcely a chapter that does not make some reference to him as suffering the torments of a lost soul. This idea of the soul being separate from the body and its development into the notion of ghosts troubling the living because there is no peace for them in death is powerfully present throughout the novel.

(A01) **PROGRESS BOOSTER**

Using appropriate critical vocabulary will enhance your grade. Make sure your references are clear and to the point. For example, when considering Brontë's use of heat as a **metaphor** to describe character, you could also reference the ways in which she uses landscape and weather as a **pathetic fallacy**, adding atmosphere and meaning to the story. For Brontë, human nature and broader nature are intimately linked.

(A04) **KEY CONNECTION**

F. Scott Fitzgerald also uses the technique of making the weather reflect the characters' emotional states and the narrative action in *The Great Gatsby* (1925) when in Chapter 5 the transition from rain to sunshine parallels Gatsby's change of mood from anxiety to hopefulness. In Philip Larkin's poem 'Talking in Bed' (1960), the restlessness of the wind echoes the gusts of emotion experienced as the couple try to find something both true and kind to say to each other.

VOLUME I, CHAPTER XII

Summary

- Catherine is genuinely ill, having starved herself and worked herself into a fever.
- Edgar is kept ignorant of Catherine's condition and spends his time reading. When he finally visits her room he finds her hallucinating and feverish and blames Nelly for her deterioration.
- Nelly discovers Isabella's favourite dog hanging from a tree, nearly dead.
- Nelly summons the doctor to attend Catherine, and the doctor informs her that Isabella and Heathcliff have been having secret nightly trysts and intend to elope.
- Isabella leaves Thrushcross Grange secretly to marry Heathcliff.
- On discovering her disappearance, Edgar disowns Isabella.

Analysis

Study focus: Nelly's role

Make sure you can write about the active role Nelly Dean plays in this chapter. She is the person who controls all the key information: Catherine's illness and Isabella's departure. Secrets are the things that move the action of the book forward, and Nelly's choice to keep them or divulge them gives her immense influence over events. Nelly's assumption that Catherine's illness is invented by her in order to manipulate others gives credence to the reading that women in the nineteenth century could use frailty as a strength. However, it is a strategy which Brontë shows to have devastating consequences.

Love and death

Secrecy is all about knowledge. Edgar is kept ignorant of Catherine's illness. Catherine does not know that Edgar is ignorant and cannot understand his apparent coldheartedness. She perceives it as a want of love. Neither Catherine nor Edgar knows that Isabella has eloped. They both perceive her absence as a lack of proper affection. This agonising perception of lovelessness immediately precedes Catherine's fervent plucking out of the feathers from her pillows. **Psychoanalytic readings** have seen this type of 'madness', identified by Nelly as a 'maniac's' (p. 129) behaviour, as both a symptom and an effect of oppression.

As Joyce Carol Oates notes in an article entitled 'The Magnanimity of *Wuthering Heights*' (*Critical Enquiry*, 1983):

> Her passion for Heathcliff notwithstanding, Catherine's identification is with the frozen and peopleless void of an irrecoverable past, and not with anything human. The feathers she pulls out of her pillow are of course the feathers of dead, wild birds, moorcocks and lapwings: they compel her to think not of the exuberance of childhood, but of death, and even premature death, which is associated with her companion Heathcliff.

In this way, the passage can be read as another allegory, another story about the story. The **anecdote** of the lapwings echoes Heathcliff's's own abandonment after his parents die, and also prefigures Catherine's grave upon the moors.

Possible readings

There are a number of other possible interpretations of this key passage. A **Marxist** or **new historicist** view would argue that mental instability is itself **ideologically** determined. The reference to the pigeon feathers connects Catherine with the ideas of natural spirituality or superstition that are in direct conflict with the dominant **discourse** of Christianity. This suggests that her 'madness', like her free spirit, is a rebellion against society and its rules.

Feminist readings of the passage may interpret Catherine's breakdown here as a condition of 'proper' femininity, the effect of domesticity and of being a wife and mother. That marriage and civilised life is not suited to Catherine is identified early on in Chapter IX, when she interprets her dream. Her pregnancy can be read as one of the causes of the arguments between Heathcliff and herself which leads her to fall ill. Her 'madness', according to such readings, is caused by the very aspects of her life that are supposed to identify her as a 'proper woman'.

Study focus: 'Madness' and imprisonment **A03**

The feminist critics Gilbert and Gubar see the madness as a result of Catherine's imprisonment. Being trapped in her marriage to Edgar thoroughly disables Catherine. She can no longer make sense of the world, sees things entirely from her own perspective, and ultimately is confined to her bed with illness. This relationship between mental breakdown and imprisonment is common to many **Gothic** tales and **Romantic** poems, notably Byron's 'The Prisoner of Chillon' and some of Emily Brontë's Gondal poems.

Key quotation: Experience and culture **A01**

When Catherine discovers that Edgar has retired to his library while she is suffering on her sickbed she is appalled: "'Among his books!' she cried, confounded. "And I dying! I on the brink of the grave!' (p. 121)

Edgar's retirement to the library after the confrontation between himself and Heathcliff, and his ignorance of Catherine's illness, can be seen as part of the conflict between experience and culture in the novel. Edgar counters his interaction with the real by submerging himself in literature. Such a critical position of course assumes that literature is not part of the 'real'. Catherine's incredulity that Edgar continues to occupy himself with his books while she is dying also highlights the discrepancy in values between the two houses of nature and culture, as represented by Heathcliff/Wuthering Heights and Edgar/ Thrushcross Grange.

Revision task 4: Mental health **A02**

Write about the way in which the deterioration of characters' mental health is depicted not just as a state of mind by Brontë but as a dysfunction of society. Focus on:

- Catherine's brain fever
- Hindley's deterioration
- Heathcliff's breakdown after Catherine's death

A04 KEY CONNECTION

This passage about the birds is also closely reminiscent of Ophelia's soliloquy in *Hamlet*, where in her mad grief she counts all the flowers. This correlation between the two texts suggests that love in characters who are as sensitive and passionate as Catherine or Ophelia can quickly slip into chaotic madness if it is not given authentic expression because of society's mores.

A05 KEY INTERPRETATION

Critical attention has focused upon the role of illness as a sign of femininity in the nineteenth century. Emily Brontë can be seen to be writing about illness as a female strategy here: rather than indicating simply weakness, illness becomes a way for Catherine to influence the actions of both Edgar and Heathcliff.

VOLUME I, CHAPTER XIII

Summary

- Catherine is diagnosed as having brain-fever and is nursed devotedly by Edgar, under whose care she slowly begins to improve.
- For two months Isabella and Heathcliff remain absent.
- Six weeks after their departure, Isabella writes to Edgar. Her letter ends with a secret pencilled note begging for reconciliation, which he ignores.
- Isabella then writes to Nelly, and Nelly now reads this letter to Lockwood.
- It says that Isabella and Heathcliff are back at Wuthering Heights (invited by Hindley who is intent on winning back from Heathcliff all the money he has lost to him through gambling).
- In the letter, Isabella perceives herself to be both friendless and abused in her relationship with Heathcliff.
- Isabella describes how Hindley showed her a gun with which he intended to kill Heathcliff. Her reaction to this weapon is one of covetousness rather than horror.
- The letter explains that Heathcliff blames Edgar for Catherine's illness and will make Isabella suffer in Edgar's place until he is able to make Edgar pay.
- The letter ends with Isabella begging Nelly to visit her at Wuthering Heights.

Analysis

Illness as metaphor

At the beginning of this chapter Catherine is sick with a fever brought on by mental anguish. Susan Sontag has written persuasively about the use of illness as a cultural **metaphor** in *Illness as Metaphor and AIDS and its Metaphors* (1991): 'Brainfever might well be thought of as the disease of someone who is a "creature of passionate extremes, someone too sensitive to bear the horrors of the vulgar everyday world"' (p. 36). Critical analysis of this chapter has focused on Catherine's entrapment in a way of life which is counter to her natural values, an imprisonment that literally makes her sick.

Isabella's inability to eat the food at Wuthering Heights because it is too coarse for her can be read as indicative of her unlikeliness to be sustained by life with Heathcliff. Like Catherine's refusal of food at the Grange it can be seen as a hostile strategy of control, in Isabella's case, punishing Heathcliff for his harsh treatment of her.

Study focus: Violent symbols

The reference to the gun, which Isabella views with desire rather than horror, is again indicative that violence is as much a part of civilised life (which Isabella has hitherto represented) as it is a part of the rude brutality of the Heights.

Feminist theorists have devoted some attention to the gun which Isabella desires, and the whip requested by Catherine at the beginning if the novel, reading both as phallic symbols. It is important to note that as phallic symbols they signify desire not for the penis as such, but for the power the penis represents. As many feminist critics have pointed out, all the economic power in the institution of marriage as it is described in this novel resides with the men.

KEY CONNECTION A04

For a collection of feminist critical essays on power in literature and society, see Mills et al., *Feminist Readings, Feminists Reading* (1989).

VOLUME I, CHAPTER XIV

Summary

- Nelly goes to see Isabella as requested and informs Edgar of Isabella's predicament, but Edgar refuses to have anything to do with his sister.
- Heathcliff determines to see Catherine whether permission is granted or not, and Nelly reluctantly agrees to act as intermediary.
- Time switches to the present. The doctor calls on Lockwood, and Lockwood reflects that he must be cautious of falling in love with the younger Catherine for fear that she might resemble her mother.

Analysis

Isabella enslaved

Isabella's position as a dependant of Heathcliff is made clear in two passages in this chapter. Firstly, Heathcliff asserts the lengths he has gone to in order to prevent Isabella claiming a separation (p. 150). In fact the effort would not have been considerable since, as John Stuart Mill notes in *The Subjection of Women* (1869), the position of women within marriage was worse than that of slaves. The second passage makes reference to Isabella's mental health (p. 151) and the practice of incarcerating women as mentally ill, despite a lack of any evidence of mental illness. Here we see Brontë's sensitivity to the ways in which power is neither generous nor neutral. It is up for grabs, and Heathcliff makes ample use of this fact, incarcerating Isabella at Wuthering Heights, keeping her isolated and apart in a separate world with special rules over which he has sole control. Isabella, in spite of her much reduced and saddened circumstances at the Heights, nevertheless displays a violent streak that subverts the expected behaviour of a woman of her status: 'The single pleasure I can imagine is to die, or to see him dead' (p. 151).

A02

Study focus: The narrators

Lockwood typically draws the wrong conclusion from Nelly Dean's story when he assumes that she is warning him against becoming too enthralled with Cathy, for Nelly sees marriage to someone else as the only escape for Cathy and is eager to find her another husband. Lockwood, once again, represents the supersensitive, precious world of the educated, or cultured, which is here contrasted with the world of passion and experience. Lockwood's illness situates him as profoundly disconnected from mundane reality, or daily life. Here Brontë cautions us against identifying too closely with the views of either **narrator**.

A01

Key quotation: 'eternally divided'

Edgar's coldness, referred to often by Catherine, emerges in this chapter as a cold-hearted indifference to his sister's plight; he refuses the more fiery emotion of anger. He says he is sorry to have lost her, but insists that communication between him and Isabella will no longer exist. Whereas Heathcliff and Catherine maintain their passionate connection, and feel that were one to die the other would inhabit a living hell, Edgar suffers no such attachment to Isabella and symbolically kills her: 'we are eternally divided' (p. 145).

A04 **KEY CONNECTION**

John Stuart Mill's *The Subjection of Women* (1869) provides an interesting, almost contemporary account of the place and role of women in Victorian society. Emily Brontë sets her novel earlier than this era, at the very end of eighteenth century, but the plight of her female characters was exactly the situation that prompted Mill to write on this issue.

A01 **PROGRESS BOOSTER**

Referring to the structural use of the two narrators to make and contrast different meanings will impress your examiner.

VOLUME II, CHAPTER I

Summary

- Lockwood takes up the **narrative** again, but speaks as though he were Nelly Dean.
- Nelly returns to Thrushcross Grange and arranges matters so that the household is empty apart from herself and Catherine, in order that Heathcliff may pay his visit.
- On seeing Catherine, Heathcliff despairs, perceiving that she is pregnant and that she is certainly going to die. The conversation and interaction between Catherine and Heathcliff ricochets between love and death, and they fall on each other in a passionate embrace, while talking of going to the grave.
- Catherine faints in Heathcliff's arms just as Edgar Linton enters. When Edgar and Nelly finally manage to revive Catherine, Heathcliff has departed but resolves to stay in the garden until Nelly can bring him news of Catherine.

Analysis

Nelly's role

Nelly is once again a catalyst for action as she traffics between Wuthering Heights and Thrushcross Grange. The narration, which throughout has properly belonged to Lockwood, as the opening to this second volume reminds us, is nevertheless more credibly Nelly Dean's.

Sexuality and death

The opening chapter of this second volume highlights the drama of the conflicts and correspondences between sexuality and death. It is possible to draw parallels between the concerns of this chapter and concerns which dominate Emily Brontë's poetry, not least the longing to escape this world, through either love or death.

Reading retrospectively, it is possible to see Heathcliff's despair upon seeing Catherine as being provoked not only by his perception of her certain death, but also of her pregnancy, since his words are 'Oh, Cathy! Oh, my life! how can I bear it?', and we only have Nelly's interpretation of his anguish as being that Catherine was 'fated, sure to die' (p. 160). Such a reading supports the **structuralist** argument that sees an association between sex and death. This is quite a complex argument but, in its most simplistic form, if sex is seen as similar to death in that it involves the absolute surrender of the body, then there is clearly a way in which Catherine's pregnancy is as abhorrent to Heathcliff as her impending death.

(A03)

Study focus: Love and money

A **Marxist** or **new historicist** reading of this chapter might look at the manner in which Heathcliff is economically transformed and the impact that this has upon his emotional relationship with Catherine. It could be argued that Catherine rejects his new persona, and her assertion 'That is not *my* Heathcliff. I shall love mine yet' (p. 161) positions Heathcliff as an opponent of, and not the embodiment of, bourgeois values.

KEY CONNECTION **(A04)**

Emily's poem 'Shall Earth No more Inspire Thee', written in May 1841, establishes an important idea that runs through her poetry and is also central to *Wuthering Heights*. This is a yearning for death in which heaven is as close to earth as possible.

VOLUME II, CHAPTER II

Summary

- Catherine's daughter Cathy is born the same night, two months prematurely.
- Catherine dies in childbirth and Edgar is so stricken with grief that he cannot welcome his daughter.
- Heathcliff knows the news even before Nelly tells him, and cries out that he cannot live without Catherine.
- The funeral takes place a week later. Hindley Earnshaw (Catherine's brother) is invited but Isabella (her sister-in-law) is not.
- Catherine is buried on a grassy slope in a corner of the graveyard nearest the moor.

Analysis

Catherine's Gothic death

Heathcliff's response to Catherine's death – that she is his life and soul (p. 169) – echoes her previous declaration of love for him in Volume I, Chapter IX. Similarly, his declaration comes just as she has departed and no action can be taken. But Brontë is at pains to demonstrate that their love **transcends** conventional boundaries, and the **Gothic** delight in ghosts and the supernatural here finds its supreme articulation in Heathcliff's declaration: 'I know that ghosts *have* wandered on earth. Be with me always – take any form – drive me mad' (p. 169). Edgar's response is to sleep, alongside his dead wife, in 'exhausted anguish' (p. 166), a sleep which seems to prefigure Heathcliff's desire to open her coffin and sleep with her in Chapter XV. Both these loves, Brontë suggests, are profound enough to extend beyond death.

Key quotation: Catherine's grave (A01)

Brontë describes the 'place of Catherine's interment' as 'outside':

> It was dug on a green slope, in a corner of the kirkyard, where the wall is so low that heath and bilberry plants have climbed over it from the moor; and peat mould almost buries it. Her husband lies in the same spot, now. (p. 170)

Catherine's burial place, almost on the moor itself, lies exactly between the two different versions of holy ground that Brontë posits in the novel: the moor and the churchyard.

She is buried beyond the plots of her families (by birth and marriage) and is therefore 'outside' their frame. This enables her to enter her kingdom of heaven (the moor) and reconnect beyond the grave with Heathcliff. Edgar chooses to be buried with his wife rather than in his family tomb, thus signifying his great love for her.

EXTRACT ANALYSIS

Volume II, Chapter II, pp. 166–9

From 'About twelve o'clock, that night' to 'He was beyond my skill to quiet or console!'

This is an important chapter, which acts as a hinge between the two volumes. The death of Catherine and the birth of Cathy enable all the structural repetitions which are such an important feature of *Wuthering Heights*.

Catherine's death highlights some important issues. Primarily, it points to the powerful nature of Heathcliff's love for Catherine, which he believes extends beyond the grave. An historicist reading of the chapter would also highlight the dangers of childbirth for women in the nineteenth century.

Nelly Dean also comments upon the consequences of Catherine's death in terms of the inheritance laws. Old Mr Linton has bequeathed his property to Isabella and subsequently to her male offspring should Edgar fail to have a son. C. P. Sanger has commented upon the very detailed knowledge that Brontë displays of the inheritance laws of the nineteenth century. This knowledge is crucial to the plot of *Wuthering Heights* since, according to this law, Cathy cannot inherit Thrushcross Grange when her father dies. Instead, the property automatically passes to the male progeny of Isabella. However, should there be no male progeny, or should that son die, the property would then revert to Cathy. It is for this reason that Heathcliff is so intent upon the marriage between Cathy and Linton, for as his daughter-in-law her property becomes his.

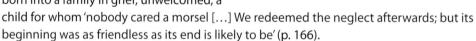

The passage starts with the birth of Cathy, born two months prematurely, and two hours before the death of her mother. Nelly describes Cathy as a 'feeble orphan' (p. 166). Scarcely any child is born in this novel without it becoming an orphan, and indeed all the mothers die apart from the surrogate mother, Nelly. This can be linked with Emily Brontë's own experience, since her mother died when she was three years old. Cathy is born into a family in grief, unwelcomed, a child for whom 'nobody cared a morsel […] We redeemed the neglect afterwards; but its beginning was as friendless as its end is likely to be' (p. 166).

Childbirth, as an experience belonging to the private sphere of womanhood, has traditionally been marginalised in literature. Here, however, Brontë focuses on childbirth as a life-changing event, indeed a life-threatening event for Catherine, resulting in her death. A **feminist reading** of this passage might focus on the impact upon identity for a woman carrying and then giving birth to a child. The bodily experience of giving birth raises questions of self and other, identity and individuality – two individuals are bound together in one body, which then divides to produce two distinct identities. Brontë highlights this unity and subsequent duality by naming both individuals Catherine. The tragic death of Catherine shortly after giving birth leaves a child without a mother, a single Cathy without her counterpart.

The second part of the excerpt details Nelly's recollection of finding Edgar Linton the next morning lying asleep next to his dead wife. This is a significant passage, for it reminds us of the strength of Edgar's feelings for Catherine, so often overshadowed by Heathcliff's. In death, they are united in an infinite calm, which is in direct contrast to Heathcliff's anguish and torment. Nelly's account sees them lying in 'Divine rest' (p. 166), as though Catherine were already an angel in heaven. While in Edgar's domain, Catherine's life (and death) is perceived as peaceful and full of propriety. This supports Edgar's decision, much later, to be buried next to Catherine on the edge of the moor.

Nelly's account of her own Christian piety in the face of death establishes Brontë's complex relationship with the conventional Victorian view of death and heaven. Nelly's account, though sentimental, is also honourable. Brontë does not ridicule the conventional view, even though she pits it against a much more robust and challenging idea of what paradise might be.

When Nelly asks Lockwood what he calls a 'heterodox' (p. 167) question about whether people such as Catherine could be happy in the other world, she identifies herself as someone who is potentially sympathetic to the possibility of the more unconventional vision being true, and it is this which makes her the ideal go-between for Catherine and Heathcliff in the previous chapters.

The next passage is one of the most dramatic exchanges between Heathcliff and Nelly, and covers Heathcliff's reaction to the news that Catherine is dead. The most striking thing to begin with is that Heathcliff already knows. He has been standing against an old ash tree, and he is so at one with it that the blackbirds (ousels) pay him no attention.

Symbolically, trees signify endurance, and balance between the spiritual and the earthly. The tree shows us how, from a tiny seed of potential, a great soul can come into being. This is entirely in keeping with Brontë's view of heaven being as one with nature. Heathcliff is at peace with the knowledge of Catherine's death when Nelly approaches him: 'She's dead! […] I've not waited for you to learn that. Put your handkerchief away – don't snivel before me. Damn you all! she wants none of *your* tears!' (p. 168).

It is only when confronted with the conventional Christian version of her death and her peace that Heathcliff flies into a passion, which causes him to bleed in agony. Brontë's account can be read as almost a crucifixion of Heathcliff. He is against the tree; he is in silent combat with his inner agony; it is as if he is 'goaded to death with knives and spears' (p. 169). His hand and forehead are stained with blood. He calls upon Catherine not to abandon him in the abyss.

Brontë also makes much of Heathcliff's animal passion in this passage, in direct contrast to the reaction of Edgar to Catherine's death, which is no less keenly felt. Heathcliff is referred to as a 'creature', 'ferocious' (p. 168), howling 'not like a man, but like a savage beast' (p. 169).

One final thing to note in this passage is Nelly's description of the moment of death: 'Her life closed in a gentle dream' (p. 169). This is extraordinary, for nowhere else in the novel are dreams referred to as gentle. Dreams are almost always disturbing and unsettling, prescient of danger or illness, and Nelly is afraid of them.

 PROGRESS BOOSTER

Watch out for key points of language that you can analyse for AO2. Here, the bestial terminology that Brontë uses to describe Heathcliff's raw pain seems appropriate to the cruelty and lack of human feeling he will display in the rest of the volume.

 KEY INTERPRETATION

Philip K. Wion's essay 'The Absent Mother in Emily Brontë's *Wuthering Heights*', reprinted in the Norton Critical Edition, has some interesting **psychoanalytical** points to make about the impact of the absent mother upon the child. It is worth paying attention to the fact that maternity, considered by the Victorians as the ultimate function of a woman, is largely her downfall in this novel, in which no mother survives.

VOLUME II, CHAPTER III

Summary

- Nelly acts as surrogate mother to the baby Cathy.
- Hindley dies shortly after Catherine, leaving the Heights mortgaged in gambling debts to Heathcliff.
- Isabella leaves Heathcliff and goes to the south of England where, a few months later, her son Linton is born.
- Heathcliff, now living alone at the Heights with the disinherited Hareton, learns of his son's birth through the servants' gossip.

Analysis

Domestic violence

The chapter begins when Isabella bursts in on Nelly at Thrushcross Grange unannounced, having run away from Heathcliff. As the **Marxist-feminist critic** Lynne Pearce points out in her essay 'Sexual Politics', when Isabella eventually flees the Heights it is indeed as a 'battered wife' (in Mills et al., 1989, p. 36). Pearce draws our attention to the very explicit nature of violence against women in this novel, arguing that it is a 'manifestation of patriarchy by force at its most extreme' (p. 36).

Isabella is en route to the south, having fled Heathcliff and the Heights. She throws her wedding ring into the fire and describes the living conditions at the Heights as both physically and morally corrupt. If we are to accept Pearce's reading, then, this jettisoning of her wedding ring is not merely Isabella's rejection of her marriage to Heathcliff, but a profound rejection of the entire oppressive institution of marriage as experienced by a relatively wealthy middle-class woman in the nineteenth century. Isabella gives a full and florid account of the violence she both witnessed and suffered at the Heights, so much so that she makes but a casual reference to Hareton hanging a litter of puppies from the chair back, whereas previously her relationship with her own dog (which Heathcliff hanged) was profound and tender-hearted.

Heathcliff's transformation

Heathcliff has now gained control of Wuthering Heights, having originally arrived as a presumed orphan, and having been humiliated by his lack of proper status. Critics have read this transformation in a number of ways.

A Marxist reading could see it as the triumph of capitalism over a belated feudalism in which competition becomes the new tyranny, since it is only through the acquisition of wealth that Heathcliff manages to move from the margins of society to its centre, infiltrating its institutions of marriage and property ownership, and appropriating them for his own ends.

A reading focused on Heathcliff as a passionate, **Romantic** figure might emphasise the fact that Heathcliff has transformed his fortunes through his passionate dedication to feeding his greedy jealousy for Catherine. Hareton, who should be the Heights' rightful inheritor, is dependent upon Heathcliff, who uses the opportunity to repeat the cruelty that he himself suffered as someone of no property or social standing.

....
The death of Hindley
....

The death of Hindley has also been the focus of much critical commentary, some of it to do with chronological correctness. Barbara Gates ('Victorian Suicide: Mad Crimes and Sad Histories' on victorianweb.org) has argued that Brontë's novel draws freely on laws and customs which post-date the setting of her story (1771–1803). In **narrating** the details surrounding Hindley Earnshaw's death (1784), for example, she draws upon statutes which relate to early Victorian customs. Although the precise cause of Hindley's death is never determined, all reports claim that he died in a state of drunkenness. Kenneth, who informs Nelly of the death, is clear and claims that he 'died true to his character, drunk as a lord' (p. 186).

Heathcliff, when Nelly asks if she may proceed with suitable arrangements for Hindley's funeral, retorts:

> Correctly ... that fool's body should be buried at the cross-roads, without ceremony of any kind – I happened to leave him ten minutes, yesterday afternoon; and, in that interval, he fastened the two doors of the house against me, and he has spent the night in drinking himself to death deliberately!
> (p. 187)

As Gates makes clear in her essay, the exact circumstances of Hindley's death, which Brontë records in considerable detail, have important implications for the course of the novel. If Hindley did die drunk and debauched, as both Kenneth and Heathcliff indicate that he did, then, according to eighteenth-century law and custom, he would automatically have been considered a suicide, exactly as Heathcliff suggests. Even more significantly, if that were to be the case his property could legally have been forfeited to the Crown, with nothing left for Hareton and hence nothing left for Heathcliff to employ as a tool in his revenge. It is therefore most likely for this reason that Heathcliff allows Nelly to perform proper burial rights for Hindley, thus relinquishing the immediate gratification of revenge upon Hindley's dead body for the larger rewards of power over the entire Earnshaw family.

 KEY CONTEXT

Burial at a cross-roads was traditional for suicides, who could not be buried in consecrated ground.

 KEY CONTEXT

In her analysis of suicides and burial customs in nineteenth-century England, Barbara T. Gates demonstrates that intimate knowledge of the laws and customs attending to death and burial has profound implications for Emily Brontë's plot.

A02

Study focus: Nelly's grief

It is worth remarking on Nelly's disproportionate grief upon hearing of Hindley's death:

> I confess this blow was greater to me than the shock of Mrs Linton's death: ancient associations lingered round my heart; I sat down in the porch, and wept as for a blood relation (p. 186).

Nelly's grief at the news of Hindley's death emphasises the tight structural pairings in this novel. Nelly and Hindley, Heathcliff and Catherine, and Isabella and Edgar all grow up in more or less fraternal relationships. Nelly's mother was in fact Hindley's wet nurse, so they did literally share 'mother's milk'. With Nelly's grief we see Brontë once again making a critical comparison between genuine heartfelt feelings of loss and grief and the formal requirements of institutionalised religion, and this scene is reminiscent of the grief demonstrated by Catherine and Heathcliff when their 'father' dies.

VOLUME II, CHAPTER IV

Summary

- Twelve years pass, which Nelly describes as being very happy ones during which she brings up Cathy, who lives a loving and protected life at the Grange.
- Edgar receives a letter from Isabella informing him that she is dying and pleading with him to care for her son. Edgar travels to see Isabella.
- During the time Edgar is away, Cathy ventures to Wuthering Heights and meets Hareton.
- Cathy is horrified to learn that Hareton is her cousin. Nelly Dean is angry with Cathy and impresses upon her that she must not inform her father of her new-found knowledge or he might order Nelly to leave his employment.

Analysis

Imprisonment

Both the Grange and the Heights can be read as confining spaces, imprisoning this new generation of Lintons and Earnshaws. Hareton is confined by Heathcliff, who has cheated him of his inheritance and has refused him any education; and Cathy is confined by the protective nature of life at the Grange, beyond whose boundaries she is not permitted to wander. Read in terms of the conflict between opposing forces, these confines can be seen as the limits of different kinds of knowledge. Hareton is forbidden knowledge of a formal, literary sort, and Cathy is prohibited from experiencing any life other than that which her father controls. When the two come into confrontation they can neither comprehend nor admit each other.

Study focus: Magic and nature

That Cathy and Hareton fail to understand each other is a source of hurt and distress for both of them, but nevertheless they do make a connection with each other, and he expands her controlled knowledge of the world by introducing her to fairy caves and 'twenty other queer places' (p. 198). Once again two opposing worlds collide, but this time Brontë holds out the promise that there can be some common ground between them in this shared love of magic and nature.

VOLUME II, CHAPTER V

Summary

- Isabella dies, and Edgar returns from the south of England with his nephew Linton Heathcliff.
- They no sooner arrive back at the Grange than Heathcliff demands Linton's presence at the Heights.
- Linton is described as a sickly and effeminate child, being delicate owing to ill health.
- Edgar is forced to promise to deliver the boy the following day.

Analysis

Pity and revenge

This chapter highlights the twin **themes** of pity and revenge. Edgar Linton does not wish to relinquish Linton to Heathcliff, but cannot find a way around it. However, his refusal to deliver the child immediately establishes something of Edgar's character. He is rational (in that he seeks a plan although he cannot find one) and he is forceful (in that he does not relinquish Linton immediately). Heathcliff's revenge requires Linton's presence at the Heights, so structurally we can see that the two themes are linked to the two houses: pity with Thrushcross Grange and Edgar; revenge with Wuthering Heights and Heathcliff.

(A02)

Study focus: Nelly's language

Notice how Nelly's language becomes more educated as she represents Edgar Linton. It is also an example of how Brontë uses the commentary of the **narrator** to articulate character. We understand something about Edgar from the form of Nelly's narration as much as from her comments.

(A01) PROGRESS BOOSTER

Consider the subtleties of Brontë's use of different language styles for each of her characters in order to promote different aspects of their personalities.

Key quotation: Linton Heathcliff **(A01)**

Our first impression of Linton Heathcliff as both feeble and an invalid frustrates conventional Victorian notions of heredity since he is Heathcliff's son. Nelly describes him as:

> A pale, delicate, effeminate boy, who might have been taken for my master's younger brother, so strong was the resemblance, but there was a sickly peevishness in his aspect, that Edgar Linton never had. (p. 200)

Linton's description links to the themes of femininity and masculinity, power and ill health, and there are also links to the wider theme of kinship and inheritance. The emphasis upon physical description suggests that he is not emotionally robust. Critics have suggested that Linton has to be sickly since he is the product of a union that should never have been and is, literally, invalid.

VOLUME II, CHAPTER VI

Summary

- Nelly takes Linton to Wuthering Heights, but this is kept secret from Cathy.
- Heathcliff professes his profound disappointment in his son, but describes his ambition for Linton to take over all the property of both the Lintons and the Earnshaws.
- In spite of Heathcliff's vindictive avarice, Nelly takes comfort from the thought that in order to achieve this aim Heathcliff must take care of his son and provide him with the education that befits a gentleman of property.
- The contrast between Linton and Hareton is starkly drawn.
- Linton repeats Isabella's inability to eat the food at Wuthering Heights (Vol. I, Ch. XIII) as it is insufficiently delicate for him.

Analysis

Progress booster: The role of food **A02**

As Philip K. Wion has noted in his **psychoanalytic reading** of the novel, *Wuthering Heights* is full of oral imagery. Almost all the social encounters involve food, and food is one of the signs of belonging and acceptance. If we persist in the reading of the two houses as representing different kinds of knowledge, then the acceptance of food represents an acceptance of a particular way of understanding life.

Food has also been seen as a sexual **metaphor**, incorporating as it does profound oral gratification. A delicate appetite might therefore be read as a reluctance to experience or engage with the sensual or the physical.

Food imagery in *Wuthering Heights*, then, operates simultaneously as the symbol of care and love, with Nelly frequently offering her charges plates of nourishing comfort food, and the instrument of control and authority. As such, it demonstrates neatly the difficulties critics have had in deciding whether this is a love story or a story of social manners. What is your view?

VOLUME II, CHAPTER VII

Summary

- Cathy's disappointment at the untimely disappearance of her cousin gives way to a resigned acceptance.
- On her sixteenth birthday she encounters Heathcliff and goes with him back to Wuthering Heights, where she sees Linton again and also meets Hareton, whom she can hardly believe is also her cousin.
- She confronts her father with her new-found knowledge.
- She learns of Heathcliff's plan for revenge and agrees not to visit the Heights again, but nevertheless conspires to find a way to correspond with Linton.

Analysis

Letters and learning

Critical attention has frequently focused on the role of letters and education in this novel, and this chapter highlights these issues. Text comes to represent knowledge, and Hareton is mocked for his lack of it or for his inability to control it. The fact that Hareton cannot read the sign above his own front door is **symbolic** of his inability to read the situation in which Heathcliff is cheating him of his rightful inheritance.

A02

Study focus: Education

This chapter highlights Brontë's view of the role of education, which is seen as both a liberator and a form of social control. This links to the **themes** of different, exclusive kinds of knowledge and power. All the characters in the novel, including its two **narrators**, are readers in one sense or another, needing to make sense of the signs before them. Hareton's lack of education is precisely what disempowers him. The route to reconciliation and resolution is through Hareton acquiring an education via Cathy.

A05 KEY INTERPRETATION

Linda Peterson (1992) observes in her introduction to a critical edition of *Wuthering Heights* that Brontë seems ambivalent about the effects of education. On the one hand, the denial of education is seen as a form of social punishment; on the other, the conventional forms of nineteenth-century education are frequently pitted against power, both sexual and physical.

A01

Key quotation: Reading the signs

In this chapter, Nelly analyses the many letters between Cathy and Linton:

> I was still surprised to discover that they were a mass of correspondence, daily almost, it must have been, from Linton Heathcliff, answers to documents forwarded by her. The earlier dated were embarrassed and short; gradually, however, they expanded into copious love letters, foolish as the age of the writer rendered natural, yet with touches, here and there, which I thought were borrowed from a more experienced source. (p. 225)

This highlights the role of the written word in the novel and links to the forbidden letters and diaries that abound throughout. It also emphasises Nelly's role as go-between and facilitator of social relationships and confirms her as an astute reader of signs, able to distinguish nuances of sophistication and the cousins' developing relationship.

A05 KEY INTERPRETATION

A **new historicist** approach would focus on these documents as evidence of the social realism of the text. L. P. Hartley's novel *The Go-Between* also makes use of this device as a means of unpicking the past.

VOLUME II, CHAPTER VIII

Summary

- The chapter opens with another distinct reference to time, and the change in the seasons. Edgar develops a chill and is confined indoors.
- Cathy climbs over a wall and cannot get back.
- While she is behind the wall she again encounters Heathcliff, who informs her that Linton is dying of a broken heart owing to her abrupt termination of their correspondence.
- Cathy's sensitive nature is deeply troubled by both this news and her fears that her father will die of his chill.
- The next day Cathy sets out again, with Nelly, to see Linton.

Analysis

Love and death

While out on the moors Cathy is morose and unable to take pleasure in the rejuvenating natural world because she is anxious about her father, and morbidly concerned with death, abandonment and whether love is enough to sustain a life. These are the primary concerns and **themes** of the novel as a whole, reiterated by Cathy in terms of filial love.

Heathcliff's information that Linton is dying of a broken heart is disingenuous. Linton is physically failing and Heathcliff wants to rekindle the love affair between Linton and Cathy – in this way he can be seen to manipulate Cathy's fear of love and death to ensure that his plans for revenge are not thwarted.

KEY INTERPRETATION (A05)

Nancy Armstrong's essay 'Imperialist Nostalgia and *Wuthering Heights*' (1982; reprinted in Linda Peterson (ed.), *Wuthering Heights*: *Case Studies in Contemporary Criticism*, 1992) has some interesting things to say about framing and enclosure in the novel.

(A02)

Study focus: Structural boundaries

This chapter includes a number of structural elements that have claimed the attention of **formalist** critics. These include boundaries, illness, death and responsibility. The door to Cathy's home is locked, and she becomes trapped behind a wall. Unable to get back over the wall, she is literally beyond the pale and therefore vulnerable to the dark forces of Wuthering Heights and Heathcliff.

VOLUME II, CHAPTER IX

Summary

- Cathy and Nelly again visit Wuthering Heights to find Linton more delicate and peevish than ever.
- Cathy and Linton quarrel about the nature of marriage, and there is a long discussion about love and whether the love between Catherine and Heathcliff was greater than that between Catherine and Edgar.
- Linton persuades Cathy to return the following day. Nelly falls ill with a chill so Cathy returns to the Heights without any supervision.

Analysis

Cathy: the hybrid

When Nelly falls ill towards the end of this chapter she comments on how well Cathy looks after her: 'like an angel' (p. 243). This links to the broader themes of good and evil, trust and deceit, and secrets in general, for in this Nelly shows an unusual incompetence at reading the signs. Cathy, however, is a true hybrid, embodying the virtues of both households, genuinely caring for the sick, but also capable of exercising her own will and judgement and going out onto the moors unsupervised.

A02

Study focus: Illness as strategy

This is another chapter in which illness is used to advance the action of the novel. Linton capitalises on his own frailty to influence Cathy's movements. Later in the chapter Nelly's chill enables Cathy to go the Heights unhindered. Illness is seen as both a form of power, a means of controlling other people, and a means to gain freedom, since Cathy makes use of the fact that Nelly is too ill to accompany her to further her own stratagem.

A05 KEY INTERPRETATION

In her book *Victorian Writing and Working Women* (1985) Julia Swindells offers an interesting account of the relationships between medicine, health and power in the nineteenth century.

A01

Key quotation: Dramatic irony

In this chapter the conversation between Linton and Cathy regarding marriage links to the broader themes of love and kinship, and who truly belongs with whom: 'Linton denied that people ever hated their wives; but Cathy affirmed they did, and in her wisdom, instanced his own father's aversion to her aunt' (p. 238). It also has a more sinister purpose, however, as Brontë uses dramatic irony to heighten the innocence and vulnerability of the children while alluding to Heathcliff's plan for revenge. Despite Cathy's 'wisdom', at this point the reader (and Nelly) knows more than she and Linton do about Heathcliff's cynical plan.

VOLUME II, CHAPTER X

Summary

- Once again the chapter opens with a distinct reference to time.
- Three weeks later Nelly is restored to health, much to Cathy's frustration.
- Nelly discovers Cathy's deception and Cathy confides in her the details of all her visits, most of which have been dutiful rather than pleasurable.
- There is a discussion about heaven between Linton and Cathy, in which she accuses his vision of being only 'half alive' and he accuses hers of being 'drunk' (p. 248).
- Hareton's attempts to read are once again the subject of mockery.
- Nelly betrays Cathy's confidence and informs Edgar of Cathy's visits, which are promptly curtailed.
- Edgar writes to Linton and invites him to the Grange.

Analysis

Knowledge and belonging

This chapter expands upon one of the central **themes** of the novel: the nature and uses of knowledge. Hareton is mocked for his limited skills; Nelly Dean uses her knowledge to influence events in the novel – her betrayal of Cathy's confidences has profound consequences for the health of both Edgar and Linton, though she is unaware of this. Critics interested in the gender issues of this novel have commented upon this emphasis on Edgar's and Linton's illnesses as serving to feminise them.

The argument about heaven is indicative of a reversal in the natures of the Grange and the Heights, since Linton's view is constricted and peaceful, and Cathy's sparkles and dances 'in a glorious jubilee' (p. 248), suggesting that neither Linton nor Cathy are where they properly belong. This also suggests that knowledge is unstable, subject to change and revision, an argument which has profound moral consequences and is one of the reasons why Brontë's novel was considered so radical and unpalatable by Victorian readers.

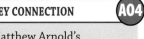
KEY CONNECTION **AO4**

Matthew Arnold's collection of essays *Culture and Anarchy* (1869) presents a prevailing Victorian notion that culture is a moral phenomenon, the ideal of human perfection, 'sweetness and light'. Although this collection post-dates Brontë, *Wuthering Heights* can clearly be considered as engaging with this idea.

VOLUME II, CHAPTER XI

Summary

- The **narrative** moves to the near present, events having only happened in the last year.
- Lockwood denies any romantic interest in Cathy.
- Edgar, realising that his death is imminent, commences a correspondence with Linton in an attempt to reassure himself as to Cathy's future.
- Linton too is dying but Heathcliff conceals this knowledge from Edgar.
- No one at Thrushcross Grange perceives Linton's health to be as precarious as it actually is.

Analysis

Letters

Once again letters play a critical and unreliable part in the sequence of events. Edgar is deceived by the letters Linton sends him into thinking that his nephew is healthier than he really is – Linton is completely under Heathcliff's command by this time. It is significant that Edgar blindly trusts the principle of correspondence to reassure himself: he is of Thrushcross Grange, the 'House of Culture'. Heathcliff, on the other hand, who has received a much shadier and darker education, is more than capable of manipulating events through a series of letters. Letters in fact suit his purposes far better than face-to-face contact, which would have been more likely to reveal the extent of Linton's deterioration.

Progress booster: Love and Lockwood **A02**

Lockwood's denial of his interest in Cathy at this point structurally repeats his account of his refusal of a 'most fascinating creature, a real goddess' (Vol. I, Ch. I, p. 6) at the beginning of the novel. His interest in women is relentlessly voyeuristic, and unrealistic. With the exception of his relationship with Nelly Dean, his interaction with women is awkward and stilted. He is frequently to be caught peeping at them through doorways or windows. Lockwood's preference for the imagined over the real relationship can be seen as participating in one of the central struggles of the novel.

Key quotation: Happiness **A01**

In this chapter, Edgar reveals to Nelly his love for his daughter: 'Ellen, I've been very happy with my little Cathy. Through winter nights and summer days she was a living hope at my side' (p. 257).

Edgar's confession that he has been happy is reminiscent of Catherine's remonstrances to Heathcliff when she is dying: 'will you be happy when I am in the earth?' (Vol. II, Ch. I, p. 160). Read in the light of this, it is not so much an acknowledgement of his love of his daughter as a confession of his insufficient love of Catherine.

A01 **PROGRESS BOOSTER**

To get the best grades at AS and A Level you need to be able to demonstrate that you understand key aspects of language and form. Consider the use of letters in this novel both as a means of moving the action along and as a **symbolic** code for establishing power.

VOLUME II, CHAPTER XII

Summary

- Cathy and Linton meet on the moors, and it is clear that Linton's health is failing.
- Cathy and Nelly are astonished and alarmed at his ill health. Linton is clearly unable to enjoy the meeting but begs Cathy to stay, and also to report to her father that she has found him in tolerable health.
- Linton is exhausted by the interchange and falls asleep.
- When he awakens he is confused and beset by voices, primarily his father's, which torment him.
- Following Nelly's inclination, they foolishly decide to keep from Edgar the extent of his nephew's ill health.

Analysis

Nelly's 'blindness'

In this chapter we are again confronted with a **narrator** who is unable or unwilling to read the signs. Nelly perceives that Linton is seriously enfeebled but permits neither herself nor Edgar that knowledge. This reluctance to acknowledge Linton's illness has disastrous consequences for Cathy and exactly reiterates Nelly's earlier fatal failure to acknowledge Catherine's malady.

KEY INTERPRETATION **A05**

In this chapter we could argue that illness is not so much used as a strategy but rather impedes the trajectory of Heathcliff's plot.

Study focus: Dreams

While he is asleep on the moors, Linton dreams that his father is calling for him and awakes in terror, 'under the spell of the imaginary voice' (p. 263). This echoes Brontë's use of the dream world to comment on the real world. What should be a tender love scene between the two cousins is fractured and disturbed by Linton's dream.

VOLUME II, CHAPTER XIII

Summary

- Cathy and Nelly repeat their meeting with Linton on the moors. This meeting, like the last, is fraught with conflict.
- Linton acts as a decoy to get Cathy and Nelly back to the Heights.
- Cathy knows that she is being manipulated by Linton, but she does not understand why.
- Heathcliff appears and is angry with Linton, who is clearly terrified.
- Heathcliff reveals that he only cares that Linton should outlive Edgar.
- Cathy and Nelly are kept prisoner at Wuthering Heights.
- Back at the Heights, Linton visibly improves and his part in the plan becomes clear.
- Cathy bites and scratches Heathcliff in her attempt to wrest the keys from him, and his response is to beat her thoroughly, much to Nelly's horror.
- Heathcliff's plan is that the two cousins should marry in the morning.
- Cathy pleads with Heathcliff to be permitted to return to the Grange and promises to marry Linton in return, but Heathcliff refuses and says that Edgar must die alone.

Analysis

A fairy-tale world?

This chapter contains many of the major **themes** of the novel: deceit, revenge, marriage, imprisonment and violence. Imprisoned at the Heights, Nelly and Catherine miss their chance of escape when three servants from the Grange come seeking them, and they are kept captive for the next four days. At this point the novel appears to recall its fairy-tale status and rehearses some of the structures of traditional fairy tales such as 'Beauty and the Beast', thus re-emphasising the oppressive nature of the marriage contract for women in the nineteenth century. Nelly reveals her legal and clerical knowledge when she reminds Heathcliff that his crime is 'felony without benefit of clergy' (p. 274).

It is worth noting that Cathy's response to the imprisonment is a reaction first of passion and resolve and then of appeal. She bites and scratches. Heathcliff retaliates with an equally violent response, slapping her about the head. She then appeals to Heathcliff to let Nelly go and inform her father, so that he may not die alone and wondering where she is: 'Mr Heathcliff, you're a cruel man, but you're not a fiend' (p. 275). The pattern of this response can be seen as being broadly allied to the two houses: a fierce reaction appropriate to the Heights, and a gentle one, more in keeping with the rules of conduct at the Grange. This is a neat demonstration of the fact that Cathy embodies both qualities and can draw on them equally.

Study focus: The role of landscape **A02**

At the beginning of the chapter Brontë describes 'a golden afternoon of August – every breath from the hills so full of life, that it seemed whoever respired it, though dying, might revive' (pp. 265–6). This is both **symbolic** and ironic. Brontë never gives us merely a literal description of the landscape. Usually such descriptions are symbolic, reflecting mood or character, using **pathetic fallacy**. Here the afternoon itself is deceiving: the hills, so full of life, first witness Linton's dramatised illness and then are the site of Cathy and Nelly's betrayal, which Cathy fears will result in her father's lonely death.

A04 **KEY CONNECTION**

Angela Carter's collection of **Gothic**-inspired fairy tales, *The Bloody Chamber* (1979), explores many of the themes of trapped maidens, violent lovers and fairy-tale landscapes that are central to *Wuthering Heights*. See 'The Bloody Chamber' and 'The Tiger's Bride' for retellings of 'Beauty and the Beast'. In the former, which is also related to the 'Bluebeard' story, the unnamed heroine escapes from her husband's castle with the help of her mother.

A03 **KEY CONTEXT**

Nelly's reference is to the system of laws which exempt clergy from civil prosecution for certain crimes. Her point here is that Heathcliff's crime is so heinous that there will be no escape clause to which he might appeal for mercy.

VOLUME II, CHAPTER XIV

Summary

- On the fifth day Nelly is able to return to the Grange where Edgar is close to death.
- Meanwhile, Cathy and Linton have married.
- Nelly informs Edgar of Heathcliff's plan and Edgar decides to change his will.
- The lawyer, bribed by Heathcliff to ignore Edgar Linton's summons, arrives too late, but Cathy arrives just in time to witness her father's dying moments.

Analysis

Inheritance laws

The complex inheritance laws of the nineteenth century are here shown to be absolutely integral to the plot. It can be argued that *Wuthering Heights* has a profoundly **feminist** agenda, since although the female characters all have power to a greater or lesser extent, they are all disempowered by the social structures of marriage, motherhood and inheritance. Since Edgar Linton fails to change his will and tie up his property in trusts, Linton is correct in his odious assumption that all Cathy's property now belongs to him (p. 280).

KEY INTERPRETATION (A05)

Miriam Allott's essay 'The Rejection of Heathcliff' (1958), in her book of critical essays on *Wuthering Heights*, is a careful analysis of our shifting responses to Heathcliff's villainy.

Progress booster: A new Heathcliff

This second volume appears to be all to do with revenge, rather than love. Our attention is once more with Heathcliff as he imprisons Cathy, insists upon her marriage to Linton and prevents her from going to her dying father. Yet these terrible acts lack the passion of his behaviour in the earlier part of the novel. It is worth considering how Brontë retains our sympathy for Heathcliff in the light of these deeds in Volume II. Largely, our response to Heathcliff is constantly adjusted and refined by our responses to the other characters: the pity we feel for Cathy and Nelly, the disgust we feel for the self-centred Linton and the complicated reaction we have to Hareton, who loves Heathcliff.

VOLUME II, CHAPTER XV

Summary

- After the funeral of her father, Cathy remains at the Grange with Nelly.
- Heathcliff arrives and, as master of the property, demands that Cathy return to the Heights, outlining his intentions to put a tenant in the Grange.
- He reveals his plans to be buried in the same space as Catherine, and tells Nelly how Catherine has haunted him over the years.
- He returns to the Heights with Cathy, leaving Nelly alone at the Grange.

Analysis

Ghosts

Heathcliff, when he arrives at the Grange to bring Cathy back to the Heights, significantly describes himself as a 'ghost' (p. 287). As he is telling Nelly how he opened the coffin to see Catherine, and plans to be buried with her so that their bodies will merge long before Edgar Linton's decomposes into them, he makes the confident assertion: 'I have a strong faith in ghosts; I have a conviction that they can, and do exist, among us' (p. 289). Heathcliff's account of Catherine's ghost and how it has haunted him over the years revises for us the absolute and unconsummated passion that marked their relationship while she was alive: he sleeps in her chamber only to be disappointed; he 'ought to have sweat blood then, from the anguish of [his] yearning' (p. 290).

Study focus: A demonic love

A04

Critical attention has focused on the transgressive nature of this chapter. Certainly, Heathcliff's description of his plan to merge with Catherine is grisly, and equally it is a plan which transgresses the boundary between life and death, and between propriety and necrophilia. As Nancy Armstrong observes in her essay 'Brontë in and out of her Time' (in Patsy Stoneman (ed.), *Wuthering Heights: Contemporary Critical Essays*, 1993), Heathcliff's plan can be interpreted as an occult dramatisation of a demonic love which utterly defies the conventions of nineteenth-century romance. This highlights a further **Gothic** strand to the novel, and connects it to the later work *Dracula* where Bram Stoker further blurs the boundaries between life and death, and desire, with his **eponymous** 'undead' vampire.

A01 PROGRESS BOOSTER

Note that the ghost of Catherine that Heathcliff summons, while disturbing, has as real a feel as any of the characters, and Brontë encourages us to believe in its reality. Even Nelly does not gainsay Heathcliff here. It is worth contrasting her reaction to Heathcliff's account of Catherine's ghost to her reaction to Catherine's attempt to tell her of her dreams in Volume I, Chapter IX.

A05 KEY INTERPRETATION

Julian Wolfreys provides an interesting account of transgression in *Wuthering Heights* in his book *Transgression: Identity, Space, Time*, Palgrave MacMillan 2008.

VOLUME II, CHAPTER XVI

Summary

- Linton dies, and Cathy is too proud to accept offers of friendship from either Hareton or Zillah, so she remains isolated at the Heights.
- Nelly Dean's story ends here, with her unable to foresee any kind of future for Cathy unless she is able to remarry.
- The **narrative** passes back to Lockwood, who reveals his intention to give up his tenancy of the Grange in October.

Analysis

Progress booster: Narrative structure

At the beginning of this chapter, Nelly tells the story in the person of Zillah, the housekeeper at the Heights. If you are studying the novel from a structural point of view, your analysis might focus on the ways in which narratives are contained within each other, for the whole of the story is Lockwood's, which encompasses Nelly's, and now Zillah's.

Unlawful inheritance

Since Linton is a minor when he dies, he cannot leave the property that he inherits by marrying Cathy to his father, but Heathcliff claims a right to it in any case. Cathy's position as a dispossessed widow radically disables her from contesting Heathcliff's command of the property and land.

Cathy and Hareton

After Linton's death, Cathy stays in her room for a fortnight but finally comes down to join the rest of the household, where she sits by the fire and reads. Hareton is entranced, both by her curls and by her reading, and asks her to read to them, a request which she angrily refuses, mistaking it for a pretence of kindness. Once again, we see Brontë setting up the relationship between her characters through misunderstanding and misreading.

Study focus: The power of death

KEY CONNECTION **A04**

See Emily Brontë's 1841 poem 'I do not weep, I would not weep', which refers to the comfort derived from a belief in the afterlife.

Cathy's response to Linton's death is that she feels dead herself: 'He's safe, and I'm free […] but […] You have left me so long to struggle against death, alone, that I feel and see only death! I feel like death!' (p. 294). This response seems to be in marked contrast to Brontë's typical response to death, which does not diminish love in any way. This suggests that for all Cathy professes to have loved Linton, the love she felt for him was weak and inauthentic. Note the stark contrast to how both Edgar and Heathcliff respond to Catherine's death.

VOLUME II, CHAPTER XVII

Summary

- The narrative returns to Lockwood and the present day.
- Lockwood takes a note to Cathy from Nelly, and reveals to Heathcliff that he has come to terminate his tenancy.

Analysis

Lockwood again

With the resumption of his narratorial position, Lockwood brings the narrative back to the present day. He agrees to take a note from Nelly to Cathy at the Heights, where once again he is rudely received by both Hareton and Cathy. Structurally, this mirrors the first chapter and completes the double arc of the narratives. Lockwood's clumsy attempt to pass Nelly's note secretly to Cathy is thwarted by her assumption that it is a love note. When she eventually learns that Nelly is the real author of the letter she is filled with reminiscent longing.

The chapter ends with Lockwood's self-conceited reflection:

> What a realization of something more romantic than a fairy tale it would have been for Mrs Linton Heathcliff, had she and I struck up an attachment, as her good nurse desired, and migrated together, into the stirring atmosphere of the town! (p. 304)

Reading and misreading

This chapter brings into focus once more Brontë's views on education, and on reading in particular. Once again, reading and misreading notes, books and situations becomes a way of establishing character and also moving the action forward. Having lost her opportunity to read Nelly's note, Cathy continues to scorn Hareton's attempts to improve his education. Hareton's response to this is a violent mix of 'mortification and wrath' which manifests itself as 'a manual check' (p. 302) (a slap on the face which splits Cathy's lip), and eventually, in distress, he throws all his books upon the fire. Brontë here reiterates the tensions and difficulties of acquiring valuable knowledge: Cathy jettisons her chance, and Hareton likewise jettisons his own, much to their individual distress.

Study focus: Lockwood's romantic dream (A03)

Lockwood's deferral of real relationships in favour of the romantic dream has already been commented upon from the first chapter where he reports his holiday infatuation with his 'goddess' (Vol. I, Ch. I, p. 6). He can only contemplate the (fairy tale) relationship with Cathy once it is clear to him that this is an impossibility. As Margaret Homans notes in her **feminist reading** of the novel: 'Lockwood's … entire narrative is predicated on romantic desires, endless oscillations of approach and avoidance' (Linda H. Peterson (ed.), *Wuthering Heights: Case Studies in Contemporary Criticism*, 1992, p. 345). As with other forms of love in the novel, it is useful to compare Lockwood's infatuation with Cathy, false or otherwise, with the central romance between Catherine and Heathcliff, and what they tell us about Brontë's views on love.

VOLUME II, CHAPTER XVIII

Summary

- The year is 1802. Lockwood happens to be in the locality again and is seized by the impulse to visit the Grange.
- He also visits the Heights where, peeping through the window, a picture of domestic bliss greets him.
- Cathy teaches Hareton to read.
- Nelly Dean receives Lockwood warmly and tells him that Heathcliff died three months earlier, a death which she describes as a '"queer" end' (p. 309).

Analysis

A successful resolution?

The **narration** now passes back to Nelly, and she describes for Lockwood the developing relationship between Hareton and Cathy. This has been conducted around learning, both in terms of Hareton's acquisition of literacy skills, and Cathy's developing humility.

Critics have tended to see this relationship between Cathy and Hareton as the resolution of all the conflicts of the novel, though opinion is divided as to whether this constitutes a successful resolution.

Study focus: The imagery of an ending

The descriptions of the landscape are full of light: 'the glow of a sinking sun', 'the mild glory of a rising moon', 'a beamless, amber light along the west' (p. 307). This use of light is **symbolic**, as Brontë sheds light on the resolution of the conflicts and struggles of the preceding chapters.

VOLUME II, CHAPTER XIX

Summary

- The narrative time moves backwards to before Heathcliff's death.
- Cathy and Hareton begin to negotiate their relationship.
- Heathcliff's will for revenge has diminished now that it lies within his power.
- Heathcliff wants to die in order to be reunited with Catherine, but feels himself to be trapped within a healthy body.

Analysis

A02

Study focus: Nature and nurture

Nelly recommences her narrative with a description of how Hareton and Cathy begin to form their friendship, and the implications that their friendship has for the political structure of the household. An **anecdote** about them digging up Joseph's prized blackcurrant bushes in order to plant flowers is indicative of Cathy's will to cultivate the garden and transform the Heights from a utilitarian place into a place for pleasure. If we see Cathy's relationship with Hareton as the resolution of the conflict between the two houses, then the planting of flowers can be interpreted as the integration of nature and culture implied in the term 'cultivation'. The flowers are described as an 'importation of plants from the Grange' (p. 317) and thus are suggestive of Cathy's own position, scion of Catherine, imported from the Grange to her truly native soil. The removal of Joseph's blackcurrant bushes indicates that his way of life must give way to a new generation. Similarly, by frivolously decorating Hareton's porridge with primroses (p. 318), Cathy moves the plain functionality of the meal into a new and celebratory dimension.

A05 **KEY INTERPRETATION**

It could be argued that under Nelly's maternal eye the Heights has been transformed into a place of sunshine and relative peace. The house is no longer barred and gated. Its boundaries have been opened up.

Heathcliff's death-wish

Cathy's newfound friendship with Hareton gives her the confidence to rebel against Heathcliff's tyranny. It is significant that this is the moment when Heathcliff's deceit might be exposed, but the love Hareton has for him stills his hand and Cathy's tongue. However, Heathcliff has abandoned his plans for revenge and now only wishes to die. The whole world seems to be constructed of memorabilia of Catherine, and Heathcliff feels trapped in a body which refuses to die, whereas his soul is already 'in the torments of hell' (Vol. II, Ch. I, p. 161). The rhetoric of this quotation has its origins in Emily Brontë's poetry.

Love and loss

J. Hillis Miller's **deconstructive** reading of the novel (*Fiction and Repetition*, 1982) focuses attention on the emphasis in this chapter upon memorabilia. He argues that each thing that Heathcliff encounters reminds him not of Catherine, but of his loss of Catherine. Like all texts, the memoranda alert us to the loss of the thing they remind us of, and not to its presence. Hillis Miller is drawing our attention to the reality gap between the world of the text and the real world. The world Brontë draws seems real but actually depicts only what is lost (not really present). Heathcliff treasures each thing that reminds him of Catherine, but despises it in equal measure because it sharpens his despair at having lost her.

VOLUME II, CHAPTER XX

Summary

- Heathcliff is obsessed with dying. His behaviour grows increasingly bizarre and he disappears for days at a time.
- When he returns, it is in a glittery, strangely joyful mood. His manner worries Nelly, who is superstitious about ghosts and the inexplicable.
- Nelly tries to convince him to make a will, and to repent of his former ways and turn to God.
- Two days later Heathcliff dies, threatening Nelly that if she does not bury his body according to his wishes he will haunt her forever.
- Hareton, who has been the most wronged by Heathcliff, is the only person who really mourns his loss.
- Heathcliff is buried according to his desires, against the opened side of Catherine's coffin.
- Local legend has it that their ghosts still walk the moors.

Analysis

Ghosts

The last chapter revisits the conflict between ethical convention and a higher morality associated with passion. Nelly wonders whether Heathcliff is a 'ghoul, or a vampire' (p. 330) and ponders again his uncertain beginnings. With no provenance, no real kinship to any of the other characters, Heathcliff becomes both like a ghost and vampiric – feeding upon the lives of ordinary people.

Almost at the end of the novel a small child, with a sheep and two lambs, encounters the ghosts of Heathcliff and Catherine as he is walking along the Nab (p. 336). This is a neutral outsider commenting on the ghosts. He is a child, he guides the lamb. These associations are all signs of his 'innocence' and therefore his 'credibility' within the story. We must believe in ghosts, according to Brontë, for they have been seen walking among us.

Study focus: Lockwood's last words

Lockwood hears the end of the story, and on walking past the graveyard on his way home pauses to wonder 'how any one could ever imagine unquiet slumbers, for the sleepers in that quiet earth' (p. 337). This reveals not only Lockwood's peculiar lack of imagination, but also his continued inability to comprehend the signs of the landscape in which he moves. Lockwood's continued incompetence as a reader of signs throws into disarray all his assumptions as **narrator** throughout the novel, causing us to reconsider his judgements.

KEY CONNECTION A04

The conflict between social convention and passion is also a central **theme** in E. M. Forster's novel *A Room with a View* (1908).

KEY CONTEXT A03

Brontë once again asserts a profound disconnect between her version of heaven and the conventional Victorian view in this chapter: 'I have nearly attained *my* heaven; and that of others is altogether unvalued, and uncoveted by me' (p. 333). This was a radical statement to make in fiction at a time when Christianity was at the heart of social values.

PROGRESS CHECK

Section One: Check your understanding

These tasks will help you to evaluate your knowledge and skills level in this particular area.

1.   Note two examples of Brontë's attitude towards and use of religion in this novel.

2.   Make brief notes on how landscape is used to establish characters in the novel.

3.   Is *Wuthering Heights* a ghost story or a love story? Write your ideas in a two-column table.

4.   Make brief notes on Brontë's use of animal imagery in this novel.

5.   How does illness operate as a **metaphor** in this novel? Write brief notes.

6.   How likeable is Heathcliff? Write a list of relevant points.

7.   How does the character of Catherine change during the novel? Write a paragraph that plots her **narrative** arc in terms of wildness and civilisation.

8.   How important is the idea of the family in this novel? Write brief notes.

9.   Identify three different ways in which Brontë uses language to establish character.

10. What is Nelly's attitude to ghosts? Find three pieces of evidence to support your answer.

11. To what extent is *Wuthering Heights* a **Gothic** novel? Make brief notes.

12. If *Wuthering Heights* is a **parable**, what idea is it illustrating? Make brief notes.

13. Discuss Brontë's use of violence in this novel. What does it suggest about character? Write your points in a two-column table.

14. Write a short paragraph on Catherine's motivations for marriage.

15. Make notes on which is more important for moving the action forward in this novel: revenge or love?

16. What does food signify in this novel? Make brief notes.

17. What is the role of education in establishing character? Identify three key characters who are shaped by education or lack of it.

18. Identify three instances where letters or books are used in the novel and make brief notes on their function.

19. What is the role of ambition in the novel? Make brief notes.

20. How important is the role of the mother in the novel? Set out your argument in bullet points.

Section Two: Working towards the exam

Below are five tasks which require longer, more developed answers. In each case, read the question carefully, select the key areas you need to address, and plan an essay of six to seven points. Write a first draft, giving yourself an hour to do so. Make sure you include supporting evidence for each point, including quotations.

1. Is *Wuthering Heights* a feminist text? Discuss with reference to at least two of the following characters: Catherine, Heathcliff, Nelly, Isabella, Linton, Edgar.

2. Compare and contrast the ways the Brontë sisters explore the relationship between education and passion for an understanding of character in *Wuthering Heights* and *Jane Eyre*.

3. Is it possible for women to be loved or does love always result in their death? Discuss the ways in which Emily Brontë and Virginia Woolf establish the fraught relationships between love, sanity and death in *Wuthering Heights* and *Mrs Dalloway*.

4. *Wuthering Heights* challenges our expectations of characters as separate and coherent individuals. Discuss Brontë's methods of establishing character with reference to at least two of the following: Heathcliff, Catherine, Cathy, Joseph, Hareton.

5. Consider the significance of religion in *Wuthering Heights* and *Tess of the D'Urbervilles*.

Progress check (rate your understanding on a level of 1 – low, to 5 – high)	1	2	3	4	5
The significance of particular events and how they relate to each other					
How the major and minor characters contribute to the action					
How Brontë uses the device of the **narrator**, given the dual roles of Lockwood and Nelly					
How Brontë structures the **narrative**					
The final outcome of the story and how this affects our view of the protagonists and the narrators					

CHARACTERS

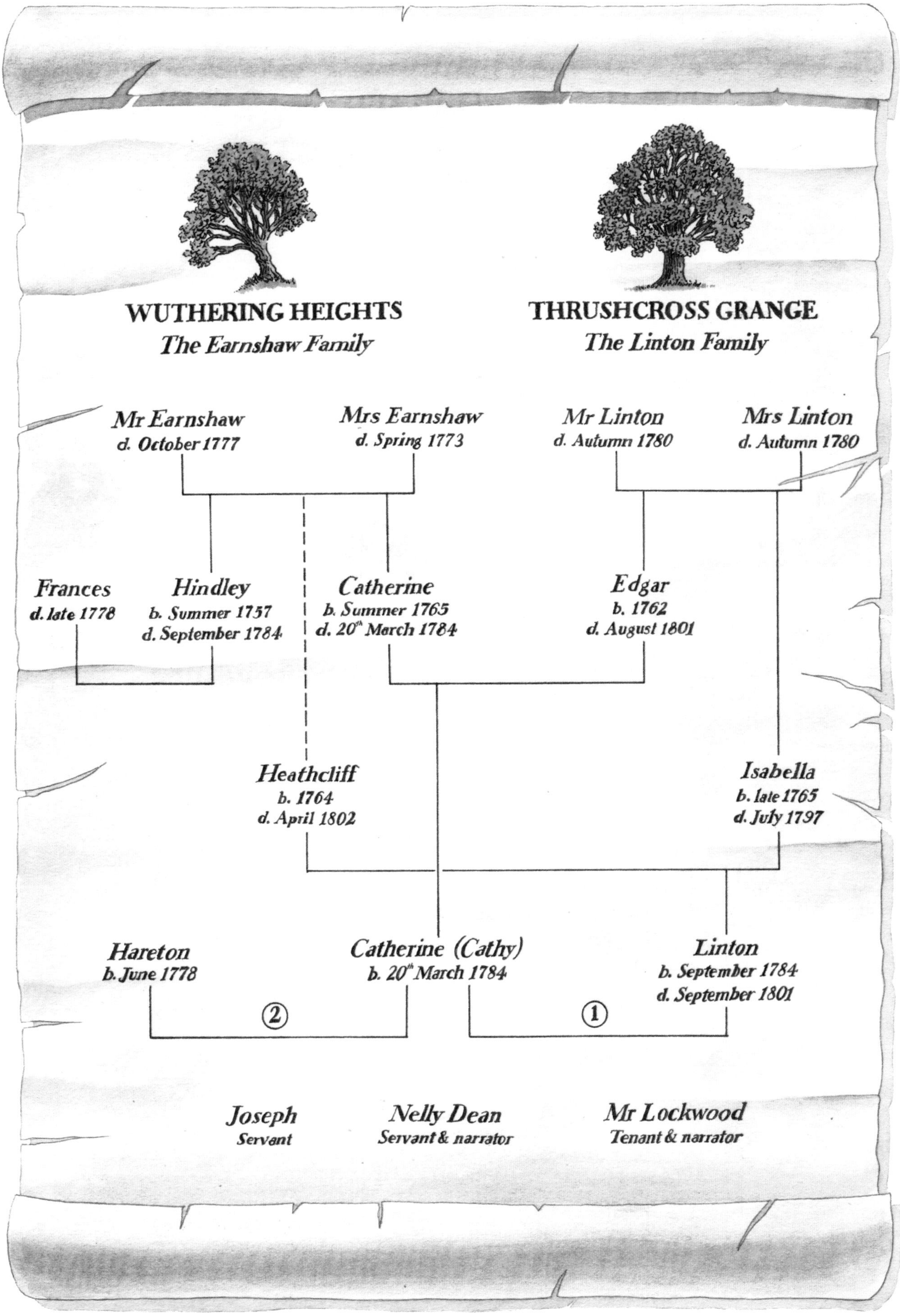

WUTHERING HEIGHTS
The Earnshaw Family

THRUSHCROSS GRANGE
The Linton Family

Mr Earnshaw
d. October 1777

Mrs Earnshaw
d. Spring 1773

Mr Linton
d. Autumn 1780

Mrs Linton
d. Autumn 1780

Frances
d. late 1778

Hindley
b. Summer 1757
d. September 1784

Catherine
b. Summer 1765
d. 20th March 1784

Edgar
b. 1762
d. August 1801

Heathcliff
b. 1764
d. April 1802

Isabella
b. late 1765
d. July 1797

Hareton
b. June 1778

Catherine (Cathy)
b. 20th March 1784

②

Linton
b. September 1784
d. September 1801

①

Joseph
Servant

Nelly Dean
Servant & narrator

Mr Lockwood
Tenant & narrator

Catherine

Who is Catherine?

- Catherine is born Catherine Earnshaw and grows up at Wuthering Heights.
- She marries Edgar Linton but passionately loves Heathcliff.
- Catherine dies after the birth of her daughter, Cathy.

Ghostly Catherine

The reader's first introduction to Catherine Earnshaw takes the form of the signature of a ghost: her name is scratched upon the window ledge in her childhood bedroom, the room where Lockwood will have his disturbing nightmares. We cannot avoid the figure of Catherine, as it is carved into the very text. At the end of the novel, Heathcliff is tormented by everything that signals to him his loss of Catherine. She is as elusive and forbidden to him as she is incomprehensible to Lockwood.

A fragmented identity

The names which Lockwood finds inscribed upon the window – Catherine Earnshaw, Catherine Linton, Catherine Heathcliff – can be read as indicative of Catherine's fractured or fragmented social identity. She struggles with conflicting ideas of herself as she tries to combine two irreconcilable lives: the life of passion fully experienced, and the life of social convention that secures her to either her father or her husband.

Study focus: Culture versus nature   A02

The conflict that disturbs Catherine's sense of self is played out in the novel through the **theme** of culture versus nature. In deciding to marry Edgar Linton, Catherine chooses culture over nature. This is directly contrasted with a **narrative** insistence upon her love of nature and her oneness with nature. As a child, for example, rather than read, she and Heathcliff prefer to scramble on the moors.
Her diary, which documents the fact, pays scrupulous attention to her jettisoning of her book but neglects to describe her impression of the moors. From Catherine's perspective, nature does not need to be named and it does not lend itself to narrative representation or to culture. If we accept this reading, then Catherine's choice of Edgar over Heathcliff cannot be expected to be successful.

Key quotation: Catherine   A01

Catherine declares to Nelly Dean: 'I *am* Heathcliff' (Vol. I, Ch. IX, p. 82).

Her assertion is both dramatic and memorable, and shows her great passion. It shows her unstable sense of identity which cannot be fixed by Heathcliff as he too is enigmatic and uncertain.

Heathcliff

Who is Heathcliff?

- Heathcliff is a foundling who is brought home by Mr Earnshaw from a trip to Liverpool, and is named after a dead son.
- He is passionately in love with Catherine, but forms no other meaningful attachments.
- He marries Isabella Linton and together they have a son, Linton Heathcliff.
- He dies longing to be reunited with Catherine.

The outsider

Unlike every other character in the novel, Heathcliff has only a single name that serves him as both Christian name and surname. This places him radically outside social patterns and conventions, and Heathcliff is described by Catherine as an 'unreclaimed creature' (Vol. I, Ch. X, p. 102), showing how he exists outside social structures such as the family. Heathcliff belongs first nowhere and finally anywhere. The fact that he inherits his name from a dead son also signals the potential for belonging and invention, since this name might be thought of as that of a ghost: a character who is no longer present.

Contradictions

As a foundling, Heathcliff is introduced into the close-knit family structure as an outsider; he is perceived as both gift and threat, and these conflicting identifications form part of the compelling undecidability of his character. Contradiction typifies Heathcliff. To Catherine he is brother and lover; to Isabella he is romantic hero and pitiless oppressor. He epitomises potency, yet he fathers an exceptionally frail child. He encompasses vast philosophical opposites: love and death, culture and nature, evil and heroism. Some critics, most notably Clifton Snider, have focused on the supernatural qualities of this novel to read Heathcliff as vampiric. Whether we read Heathcliff as monstrous or as a **Byronic hero**, he disturbs the conventional structure of the novel, and of the world created within it.

Study focus: A Byronic or Romantic hero **A03**

Critics have most often cited Heathcliff as a Byronic hero: powerful, attractive, melancholy and brutal. Through most of the first volume of the novel Heathcliff's rise to power details the ascension of the **Romantic** hero, with his intrusion into and transformation of a conventional and socially limited world. However, by making such romantic conventions manifest in an energetic new form, Heathcliff actually cancels out Romantic possibilities and reduces that system to mere superstition. Thus in creating Heathcliff, Brontë may well have been acknowledging Byron's influence. But in the character of Catherine she also suggests a revision of Byron and demonstrates his vision as a fundamentally male literary myth.

Key quotation: Heathcliff **A01**

Catherine warns Isabella about Heathcliff when she says: 'He's not a rough diamond – a pearl-containing oyster of a rustic; he's a fierce, pitiless, wolfish man' (Vol. I, Ch. X, p. 103). He is uncivilised, and even love will not tame him. The fact that this assessment comes from Catherine, who loves him, means that we treat it seriously.

A05 **KEY INTERPRETATION**

When we meet Heathcliff as a child, the things we find out about him are that he is capable of enduring anything (Vol. I, Ch. IV, p. 38) and that he has a profound connection with Catherine. These two characteristics remain with him throughout the novel, and are what enable him to achieve his ends.

A03 **KEY CONTEXT**

The description 'Byronic' means characteristic of or resembling Byron or his poetry: that is, contemptuous of and rebelling against conventional morality. Lord Byron (1788–1824), the most flamboyant and notorious of the Romantic poets, created the idea of the Romantic hero: unruly, melancholy and haunted by secret guilt. It is clear that in many ways Heathcliff typifies this description.

Edgar

Who is Edgar?

- Edgar Linton is heir to Thrushcross Grange and Isabella's brother.
- He loves, and marries, Catherine Earnshaw, and together they have a child, Cathy.

The child

Edgar's world is an interior world, and we first see him as a child, poetically pictured by Heathcliff for Nelly Dean. Edgar's world is:

> a splendid place carpeted with crimson, and crimson-covered chairs and tables, and a pure white ceiling bordered by gold, a shower of glass-drops hanging in silver chains from the centre, and shimmering with little soft tapers (Vol. I, Ch. VI, p. 48).

In the midst of this sumptuous environment, the description of which sits so uncomfortably in Heathcliff's mouth, stands Edgar, weeping by the fire. And Heathcliff despises him for his pettiness. From our first introduction to Edgar we perceive him to be emotional and Heathcliff describes him and his sister Isabella as 'petted things' (Vol. I, Ch. VI, p. 48).

Lacking spirit

As a man, Edgar Linton is described as lacking spirit, and this can be read in two ways. Conventionally, he does lack the vigour that characterises Catherine and Heathcliff. However, he also lacks their ghostliness, the spectral quality which sets them apart and lends them mystery. By comparison, Edgar's physicality is easy to read. He is not troubled by internal contradiction, and he remains in his place throughout the novel, living at Thrushcross Grange as boy and man, and finally resting in his grave alongside the body of his wife.

Study focus: Masculine or feminine?

It is rather a commonplace of criticism to read Edgar as effeminate, in contrast to the savage masculinity of Heathcliff. Critics interested in the gender issues of the novel have commented upon the emphasis on Edgar's and Linton's illnesses as serving to feminise them. The **feminist critics** Gilbert and Gubar (*The Madwoman in the Attic: The Woman Writer and the Nineteenth-Century Literary Imagination*, 1979) have reversed this trend, however, reading Edgar as masculine and Heathcliff as feminine. Edgar's masculinity, they argue, is that of social power. He legitimately inherits Thrushcross Grange; his books and his library establish him as a man of letters and therefore of influence. Nelly's constant reference to Edgar as 'the master' reveals her opinion of him as someone with social power.

Key quotation: Edgar A01

Catherine describes Edgar as a character type: 'Your type is not a lamb, it's a sucking leveret' (Vol. I, Ch. XI, p. 115). By this Catherine means that Edgar is weaker than a lamb. As an unweaned hare, he would be prey to every predator.

Edgar is in need of love and protection. It is significant that this outburst comes in the middle of an argument between Edgar, Heathcliff and Catherine.

Isabella

Who is Isabella?

- Isabella is Edgar Linton's sister.
- She falls in love with and marries Heathcliff, much against Catherine and Edgar's advice.
- Edgar disowns her and Heathcliff treats her cruelly.
- Realising her mistake, she flees Heathcliff and moves to the south of England, where she lives for the rest of her life.
- While in the south of England she bears Heathcliff's son, Linton Heathcliff.
- Isabella dies when Linton is twelve years old.

A vixen or a dove?

Isabella is frequently referred to with animal imagery. In Volume I, Chapter X, she is likened to a monkey, a little canary, a sparrow's egg, a cat, a tigress, a vixen and a dove. The characteristics of these animals serve to demonstrate her complex nature, a mixture of helplessness and ferocity. Ultimately, she will be destroyed by the forces that range against her, but given the insistence upon the animal imagery throughout her characterisation, we are encouraged to read this as part of nature, and a natural consequence of her personality and the choices she makes.

Study focus: Isabella's characterisation (A05)

As she is Edgar's sister, Isabella's characterisation is closely associated with his. Indeed, she is only ever seen in relation to other characters. Isabella's attachment to Heathcliff, which structurally parallels Edgar's fascination with Catherine, fails to develop into a mature and unselfish love. Her infatuation with Heathcliff is a direct result of her cultural life: she can only read Heathcliff as a **Romantic** hero, and she never entirely abandons her fantasy of Heathcliff as the **Byronic** lover, even when it is clear that his spontaneous love of Catherine has transformed itself into a determined lust for revenge, for which Isabella is only a cipher or vehicle. Feminist critics, looking at the novel from the perspective of **gynocriticism**, have devoted their attention to the brutal realities of Isabella's position as a battered wife, and have theorised the power relations that seem to make her complicit in her oppression.

Key quotation: Isabella (A01)

Catherine describes Isabella to Nelly Dean, noting 'the brightness of Isabella's yellow hair, and the whiteness of her skin [...] her dainty elegance, and the fondness all the family exhibit for her' (Vol. I, Ch. X, p. 98).

This description is significantly inanimate. Isabella appears like a portrait of herself, or a doll, not a person. There are similar descriptions of Edgar and this account of the Lintons emphasises their civility and status.

(A03) KEY CONTEXT

Darwin's *On the Origin of Species* (1859), which outlines his theory of evolution and the survival of the fittest, was a key work in the nineteenth century. Notions of strength and who is fit to rule underpin the social structure of this novel.

(A05) KEY INTERPRETATION

See Sheryl Mann's essay 'In Defense of Isabella Linton: An Analysis of her Role in *Wuthering Heights* as a Foil to Catherine Earnshaw' (2012).

Linton

Who is Linton?

- Linton Heathcliff is the son of Isabella Linton and Heathcliff.
- He is Cathy's first cousin.
- For the first twelve years of his life he lives in the south of England but he moves to Yorkshire when his mother dies.
- Edgar Linton wishes to look after him at Thrushcross Grange, but Heathcliff prevails and Linton is sent up to the Heights to live.
- Linton and Cathy marry, in spite of Linton's ill health.

A contradiction

Linton Heathcliff is a contradiction in terms. His name signifies the unnatural union between Heathcliff and the Lintons, or between passion and convention, and his sickly nature demonstrates the impossibility of such a union. In Linton, love and convention emerge as corrupted by each other. Like both his parents, however, Linton's view of the world is singular, and it is his inability to see it in any but his own terms which renders him absolutely available for manipulation by Heathcliff.

Study focus: Gender ambiguity

It is possible, following Gilbert and Gubar (*The Madwoman in the Attic: The Woman Writer and the Nineteenth-Century Literary Imagination*, 1979), to read Linton as an example of the gender ambiguity with which Brontë imbues her characters. Linton displays many of the characteristics that a Victorian readership would be used to associating with typically female characters: he is manipulative, fickle, sickly, babyish – 'sucking a stick of sugarcandy' (Vol. II, Ch. XIV, p. 279) – and enfeebled in his relationship to dominant characters.

Key quotation: Linton

Brontë reserves for Linton her most scathing imagery: he is described as 'a pet' (Vol. II, Ch. V, p. 201), a 'puling chicken' (Vol. II, Ch. VI, p. 207), and a 'whelp' (Vol. II, Ch. VI, 208).

The animal imagery establishes Linton Heathcliff as both immature and less than human.

Hareton

Who is Hareton?

- Hareton Earnshaw is the son of Hindley and Frances Earnshaw.
- He is left to run wild, ill-educated and ill-treated.
- At the end of the book, he and his cousin Cathy Linton are planning to marry.

Love

Hareton's relationship with Cathy has been read as mirroring Heathcliff's with Catherine, in that he wants to impress her, and is proud in her presence. His love of Cathy can be seen to resemble Edgar's love of Catherine, being moderate yet tender, devoted yet restrained. Hareton also exhibits an unwavering love for Heathcliff, in spite of the ill-treatment he has received at his hands. Like Catherine, Hareton is constant in his initial affections, and when Heathcliff first arrives in his life they form an alliance against Hindley. Hareton's physical resemblance to Catherine complicates Heathcliff's relationship with him. Heathcliff loves Hareton in spite of himself, saving his life as a baby and, at the end of the novel, relinquishing all that he has to him.

Education

Hareton's characterisation revolves around his education. He is initially nursed by Nelly, and with her he begins to learn his letters. However, left to the care of his dissolute and unpredictable father, Hindley, Hareton grows wild, unable to read, and with no social skills. His attempts at self-improvement are a source of derision for Linton and Cathy. It is not until the end of the novel that he is able to acquire the skills necessary for him to achieve social equality with Cathy and come into his rightful inheritance. He is taught these skills not without some diminution of his sexual potency, as he sits meekly to be alternately kissed or chastised as he learns. The domestic romance which marks the union between Cathy and Hareton may resolve some of the conflicts that thwart the other relationships in the novel, but nevertheless lacks the power of the original love between Catherine and Heathcliff.

Study focus: Inheritance **(A02)**

Although Hareton's name is inscribed above the door of Wuthering Heights, his inability to read, coupled with the doubling of names and signatures, means that initially he fails to inherit his rightful property. Inheritance requires a stable system of patriarchal legitimacy and uncontested identity. Hareton is at first dispossessed by Heathcliff, but can also be seen as a rewriting of Heathcliff: a surrogate or **symbolic** Heathcliff. He is finally able to repossess the Heights, only to be immediately assimilated into the cultural **hegemony**, or authority, of the Grange.

(A05) KEY INTERPRETATION

Among those of his generation, Hareton's character is perhaps the most intriguing, reversing the comparative lack of interest we feel for his father, Hindley. Hareton is brutalised by Heathcliff, structurally repeating Heathcliff's own suffering at the hands of Hindley. His character resolves many of the contradictions in the novel, combining the qualities of both houses: the energy and spirit of the Heights with the willingness to please and gentleness of the Grange.

Key quotation: Hareton **(A01)**

Cathy kisses Hareton and makes him a present of a book, and 'He trembled, and his face glowed – all his rudeness, and all his surly harshness had deserted him' (Vol. II, Ch. XVIII, p. 314). This is an example of how Brontë uses the synthesis of nature and culture, passion and civilisation to resolve the conflicts of the novel. The instinctive kiss and the accompanying gift ennoble Hareton, and prompt the reconciliation between him and Cathy. It is significant that the romance of the magic kiss is, by itself, insufficient to redeem Hareton. Before the two houses can achieve harmony, he must accept the gift of the book.

Cathy

Who is Cathy?

- Cathy Linton is the daughter of Catherine and Edgar Linton.
- She is cousin to Linton Heathcliff and Hareton Earnshaw.
- She is brought up in a protected environment at the Grange until she meets Hareton and discovers the world beyond the Grange.
- She marries Linton Heathcliff, and when he dies she continues to live under Heathcliff's tyranny at the Heights.
- She forms a powerful and redemptive relationship with Hareton and by the end of the book is planning to marry him.

A romantic conclusion?

The novel records Cathy's pride, and her insensitive mockery of Hareton's lack of formal knowledge. The resolution of the novel in which she and Hareton form their attachment is something of a mythical resolution, a romantic conclusion which **transcends** the central conflicts of the novel to restore a traditional novelistic plot of courtship and marriage. Cathy and Hareton's relationship restores to the novel a version of domestic bliss that was the Victorian ideal, but it is well to bear in mind that Brontë's is a version in which Cathy clearly has the upper hand.

Key quotation: Cathy

Cathy is described by Nelly as 'the most winning thing that ever brought sunshine into a desolate house – a real beauty in face – with the Earnshaws' handsome dark eyes, but the Lintons' fair skin, and small features, and yellow curling hair. Her spirit was high, though not rough, and qualified by a heart, sensitive and lively to excess in its affections ... her love never fierce; it was deep and tender' (Vol. II, Ch. IV, p. 189).

This character reference from Nelly is striking, and it influences the way we reflect upon the sour behaviour of Cathy Heathcliff as she presents herself in the first volume of the novel.

Nelly is here speaking to Lockwood, whom she sees as a possible escape route for Cathy, should he be induced to fall in love with her.

Progress booster: Cathy and Catherine

Structurally, the second Cathy can be seen as revising her mother's story. She achieves her identity at the price of her mother's, given that Catherine dies in giving birth to her, and Edgar always differentiates her in relation to the first Catherine, whose name he never shortened. Unlike Linton, who has the misfortune of inheriting the worst of both his parents, Cathy appears to have inherited the good from both of hers. Cathy embodies her mother's capacity for fierce attachments, but her relationship with Hareton, which resolves the central conflicts of the novel, lacks the destructive power of Catherine's with Heathcliff.

Nelly

Who is Nelly?

- Nelly Dean is the second and the dominant narratorial voice in this novel.
- In keeping with her dual roles (narrator and character), she has two names: Nelly, which is used by her peers and familiars, and Ellen, which is used as a mark of respect.
- She is servant to both houses during the course of the novel.
- She acts as a mother figure to most of the characters in the novel, including Lockwood, the other **narrator**.

Study focus: Dual role **A02**

It is important that you can write about Nelly's dual role in the text. As narrator, Nelly Dean takes up the story from Lockwood and gives it both substance and credence. Lockwood's inability to read the signs of the culture in which he finds himself cannot sustain the story, though it acts to remind us that all narratorial voices, including Nelly's, are partial or biased. As a narrator, she might be read as being the 'servant' of the text, since she brings it to us and provides us with an explicatory commentary. Nelly Dean is a local, and has known each generation of the Earnshaw and Linton families. She is therefore well placed to offer Lockwood a commentary upon the events she describes. Her position as a servant in the household is differentiated from that of the other servants, both in terms of her ability to move effortlessly between the two houses, mediating between their differences, and in terms of her voice. She also emerges as an educated woman, having read most of the books in the library at Thrushcross Grange – the house of culture; she has also experienced the vicissitudes of life at Wuthering Heights – the house of nature.

Language and dialect

Nelly Dean is one of the most interesting characters in the novel, not least because of the language she uses. Both **feminist** and **Marxist critics** have acknowledged that in looking at literary texts it is important to consider the way in which women's access to language and education is **ideologically** determined. Nelly Dean, however, occupies a unique cultural position in this novel. Nelly Dean does not share a regional **dialect** with the other servants, although she understands it perfectly well. She has access to a range of **discourses** that might be considered 'beyond her ken' in terms of her position as a family servant; yet as the central narrator, she is presented by Brontë as a speaking subject, partially excluded from culture but nonetheless positioned so as to be able to comment upon it.

Surrogate mother

Nelly acts as a surrogate mother to many of the motherless characters in this novel: she brings up Hareton for the first five years of his life; she cares for Cathy from birth through to her marriage to Linton; she regrets the brevity of her charge of Linton Heathcliff, which is forced by circumstance; and she acts as confidant and adviser to Catherine and Heathcliff. She also acts as a mother figure to Lockwood as she nurses him back to health. As surrogate mother, Nelly provides food and moral sustenance to her nurslings. Q. D. Leavis, writing in the 1930s, has this to say of Nelly Dean: 'Nelly Dean is most carefully, consistently and convincingly created for us as the normal woman, whose truly feminine nature satisfies itself

---

A04 | **KEY CONNECTION**

In *Wuthering Heights*, Nelly Dean offers practical advice, emotional reassurance and physical assistance to the main characters, most of whom would otherwise lack a mother-figure in their lives. In *Jane Eyre* (1847), Jane is also orphaned and similarly encounters a series of strong women to whom she can turn for maternal support and comfort, in the shape of Miss Temple and Mary and Diana Rivers, all of whom are well educated and sympathetically portrayed.

A01 | **PROGRESS BOOSTER**

Being able to identify the different ways in which Nelly uses language will enhance the quality of your essays.

Marina Warner observes in her analysis of fairy tales that: 'The goose was sacred to the Goddess of Love, Aphrodite' (*From the Beast to the Blonde*, 1994, p. 51). This notion of Nelly as the servant of love is supported by the way she moves freely between the two houses.

in nurturing all the children of the book in turn' (reprinted in Stoneman (ed.), *Wuthering Heights: Contemporary Critical Essays*, 1993, p. 28). Contemporary **feminist critics** may take issue with this conflation of essential feminine nature and maternity, but this was certainly the **ideology** of the day for Victorian readers.

This reading of Nelly as a mother figure alerts us to another of her roles, for Nelly is a Mother Goose, the teller of this fairy tale, the keeper of its wisdom. The name might also be a corruption of Mother Gossip. Both of these definitions are pertinent to the figure of Nelly, since the knowledge she conveys is at least twofold: it is about women's experience, and it is about the nature of love.

Lockwood

Who is Lockwood?

- Lockwood is one of the main **narrators** of the novel.
- His voice is that of an educated man, though his tone, from his diary entry, is confiding and self-important.
- His dreams at Wuthering Heights form one of the centrally important aspects of the novel.

Narratorial perspective

Employing the double **narratives** of Lockwood and Nelly was a highly original technique, permitting Brontë to comment upon the nature of narratorial perspective. This technique also alerts us to the fact that different kinds of knowledge, and different kinds of world view, compete with each other for precedence in this novel. Lockwood's narrative is more self-consciously literary, written almost as a diary entry, a written account; Nelly's is an oral, storytelling narrative, more intimate and more dramatic in tone, drawing us into the world of the novel. Nelly's is a narrative of original immediacy, contrasted with Lockwood's complex, Latinate and florid style, given to many sub-clauses and adjectives.

Joseph

Who is Joseph?

- Joseph is a lifelong servant at Wuthering Heights.
- He provides the least accessible form of Yorkshire **dialect**, situating his character as intransigent.
- He represents a hard-line traditional religious view, which is unflinchingly judgmental.

Language and character

From the first chapter we see Lockwood through his diary entry. We get an impression of him through his language, not a physical description. When we meet Joseph, our impression of him is formed through his speech. The first thing Joseph says is simple and biblical – 'The Lord help us!' (Vol. I, Ch. I, p. 4) – and then we immediately hear his colloquial, mumbling, almost unintelligible **dialect**. There is a minimum of physical description, and this contributes to an emphasis on emotion. We may not understand Joseph, but we learn to 'read' his emotional character very quickly.

THEMES

Love

Wuthering Heights has been called the greatest of love stories, and the love story is indeed central to the novel. This is a novel that explores love from a number of different perspectives: domestic, maternal, social, romantic, religious and **transcendent**. But it is also a novel which explores that **theme** through a range of conventions which startled and confused its contemporary readership, and still causes us to reflect on our conventional notions of what constitutes the **genre** of the love story. In the central relationship between Catherine and Heathcliff, Brontë takes the sweep of idealised romance, for example, and fuses it with **Gothic** fantasy and horror. In the comfortable domestic realism of Catherine's marriage to Edgar, Brontë interleaves a theme of illness and childbirth which eventually leads to death.

Fantasy characterises the relationship between Isabella and Heathcliff, and similarly that between Catherine and Edgar. They love in the other something they cannot achieve for themselves. By contrast, it can be argued that narcissism (extreme love of oneself), characterises the relationship between Heathcliff and Catherine.

A02

Progress booster: Love and violence

It is essential that you can write about how love and violence are linked in the novel. When Heathcliff's love of Catherine corrupts into a lust for revenge, his passion transgresses powerful social taboos: he lies with her dead body in the grave; he tyrannises his dying son in order to accumulate wealth; and he torments his wife without compunction. Catherine, unable to reconcile her passion for Heathcliff with her marriage to Edgar, resorts to self-destruction: 'I'll try to break their hearts by breaking my own' (Vol. I, Ch. XI, p. 116). She refuses food, wilfully exposes herself to a chill when she is feverish, and works herself up into a nervous agitation while she is carrying Edgar's child. She dies in childbirth, and her daughter is born two months prematurely. The greatest of love stories, then, is explored through the profoundest acts of violence.

Nature and culture

The dichotomy between nature and culture, which forms part of the thematic structure of this novel, is played out in the relationship between the two houses: Wuthering Heights, which represents nature, and Thrushcross Grange, representing culture. The theme is developed in the ways in which the houses similarly represent enclosure and exposure. The opposition between these two displays them as both antagonistic and subtly matched. This is a conflict that can be interpreted in a number of ways: in historical terms, as a rural way of life contends against industrialisation; in psychological terms, as a struggle between the ego and the id; in sexual terms, as a choice between experience and representation.

The descriptions of nature in this novel are almost never gratuitous, or simply scene-setting. They have a **symbolic** significance so it is worth paying attention to them. From the very beginning Lockwood identifies himself as a man of culture, appropriately living at the Grange, and utterly incapable of reading the signs of nature. His abortive attempt to negotiate the snowstorm and read the human signs which underlie the elements are testimony to this.

Gilbert and Gubar's essay on *Wuthering Heights* (in *The Madwoman in the Attic*) sees the opposition of nature and culture in traditionally gendered terms, with culture as male and nature as female. Indeed, they assert that this novel is 'gender-obsessed'. Within the novel, a reading of the gendering of nature as female is supported by the manifestation of the storm as a female witch-child, the original Catherine, in Lockwood's second visionary dream. Heaven and hell are seen in similarly gendered terms. Catherine's choice of culture over nature, in marrying Edgar, is overlaid by her assertion that she has 'no more business to marry Edgar Linton than I have to be in Heaven' (Vol. I, Ch. IX, p. 81).

Professor John Bowen has produced a series of instructive video essays, published by the British Library, on *Wuthering Heights* which are available at www.bl.uk/romantics-and-victorians. In his piece on nature and culture ('Walking the Landscape of *Wuthering Heights*') he remarks that in an early essay, Brontë sees nature as essentially destructive and indifferent to human purposes and needs, which is arguably at odds with her view of it in *Wuthering Heights*.

Nature is neither legible nor representable in this novel. Lockwood cannot read its signs, and Catherine refuses to name it. Nor is nature seen as unremittingly cruel in comparison to culture. The representations of culture show it as equally dangerous, and violent, and there are descriptions of the natural world which are tender and refined. The novel opens with Lockwood's account of the countryside and his impression of his place within it:

> This is certainly a beautiful country! In all England, I do not believe that I could have fixed on a situation so completely removed from the stir of society. A perfect misanthropist's Heaven – and Mr Heathcliff and I are such a suitable pair to divide the desolation between us. (Vol. I, Ch. I, p. 3)

Lockwood inhabits the landscape of the moors as a tourist. As a tourist, he is a consumer, converting the landscape and the lives of its occupants into a private aesthetic experience. He contributes nothing to its maintenance; he fails to understand its dangers or even to read its beauty except in a romanticised and sentimental way. In Nancy Armstrong's essay 'Imperialist Nostalgia and *Wuthering Heights*' (in Linda H. Peterson (ed.), *Wuthering Heights: Case Studies in Contemporary Criticism*, 1992), she argues that:

> Lockwood's journey into the wastelands, farms and villages is a journey back in time. As the story regresses through preceding generations of the Earnshaw family, it appears to be taking us back to the primitive beginnings of the culture (p. 435).

Key quotation: Savagery and civilisation

When Catherine is ill and she berates Nelly for having contributed to her illness, she is referring to Nelly's advice that she should marry Edgar. 'Nelly, *you* have helped to unsettle me! […] Oh, I'm burning! I wish I were out of doors – I wish I were a girl again, half savage and hardy, and free … and laughing at injuries, not maddening under them! Why am I so changed?' (p. 125)

Links can be drawn here to the wider **themes** of nature versus culture, savagery versus civilisation. Catherine's words refer to the fusion between self and landscape that characterises Catherine and Heathcliff. The reference to childhood also suggests that their relationship is essentially 'innocent'.

Progress booster: Nature and the author

In *Wuthering Heights*, Emily Brontë employs landscape imagery in particular to represent heightened emotional states that would otherwise defy representation in the nineteenth-century novel. Even though the emotions were couched in more or less poetic language, this novel caused such a public outcry upon publication that Charlotte Brontë was required to defend it. Her defence consisted of situating her sister precisely in the nostalgic rural environment that cannot be held responsible for its actions. In other words, Emily Brontë, writing in an isolated rural environment, more or less dislocated from the refined social mores of urban life, could not have predicted the outrage her novel would cause. This was, of course, disingenuous of Charlotte but is indicative of the radical departure *Wuthering Heights* represented from what Victorian readers had been led to expect.

To identify Emily with the region that she represented, Charlotte infused her with nostalgia. She reframed the novel as something 'rustic all through. It is moorish and wild, and knotty as the root of heath.' Charlotte's preface claimed these same qualities for its author: 'nor was it natural that it should be otherwise, the author being herself a native and nursling of the moors' (p. li).

The representation of nature

This relationship between landscape and the emotions can be read in both directions. Margaret Homans, in her essay 'Repression and Sublimation of Nature in *Wuthering Heights*' (in Juliann E. Fleenor (ed.), *The Female Gothic*, 1983) takes up a point first made by Leo Bersani about the destructiveness of nature. Pointing out that nature is hardly ever directly represented in this novel which appears to be about nature, Homans argues that Emily Brontë chooses indirect methods such as **metaphor** or **anecdote** as a mode of repressing nature's more threatening aspects.

Revision task 5: Brontë's representations of nature **A02**

Write about the way in which Brontë depicts nature both literally and figuratively in the novel. Focus on:

● The depiction of the moors, both in terms of their importance to individual characters and how they reflect mood and/or themes

● How animal imagery is used at particular moments or for particular characters

Property and ambition

While we could argue that *Wuthering Heights* is first and foremost a tale of passionate relationships expressed through and reflected in the wild, natural landscape, more worldly aspects also play their part. As Heathcliff turns his anger into a desire for revenge, his ambition for power and property also becomes a driving force in the novel.

Study focus: Inheritance

Note how Heathcliff is able to obtain control of both properties through his clever manipulation of the complex laws of inheritance. When Mr Earnshaw dies there is no mention of a will. Catherine and Hindley therefore inherit all the personal property equally and Wuthering Heights passes to Hindley. Catherine's personal property passes to Edgar upon marriage. Hindley gambles his inheritance away, and on his death it emerges that Heathcliff is the mortgagee of the Heights, so the property is his. The Linton property is different. It has parkland, and is much more of an estate property. In his will, Mr Linton leaves the property to Edgar, his only son. Edgar's daughter is passed over in favour of Mr Linton's grandson (Isabella and Heathcliff's son). Heathcliff has no legal right to the property, but he claims the right on behalf of his son and his wife. Heathcliff thus comes into possession of both properties.

A04 KEY CONNECTION

Writing Worlds: Discourse, Text and Metaphor in the Representation of Landscape, edited by Trevor J. Barnes and James. S. Duncan (1992), offers a range of insightful essays focusing on the representations of landscape within a variety of texts, which would powerfully inform your reading of landscape in *Wuthering Heights*.

A03

Morality and education

Morality

There are at least three views of morality which are pitted against each other in this novel. Conventional, institutionalised morality might be said to be most forcibly represented by Joseph, and it is shown as pious, restrictive, domineering and legislative. Ever ready with a biblical quotation or religious homily, Joseph provides a relentlessly sour commentary upon the activities of the other members of the Heights household. His is the restrictive voice of social convention which intrudes upon this house of nature, regulating it and judging it.

The second form of morality which is explored in the novel focuses attention upon the morality of authenticity, of being true to the self. In the light of this morality, Catherine's marriage to Edgar is judged as an extreme act of bad faith which precipitates all subsequent tragedy and evil.

The third form of morality which is explored is that of self-interest over altruism. Many of the characters in the novel appear to act for the good of others, and yet their actions serve the aggrandisement of their own power or knowledge. For example, Nelly Dean withholds or reveals her knowledge apparently arbitrarily, but her choices to do so invariably influence the events of the novel. Examples of this are when she neglects to tell Edgar about Catherine's illness and when she informs him of Cathy's correspondence with Linton. On each occasion her decision has profound consequences for the events of the novel.

Education

Brontë seems ambivalent about the effects of education. The denial of education to Heathcliff is perceived as a form of social punishment and humiliation. It robs Heathcliff of status both within the family and within society. Yet Hareton's painful acquisition of a formal education in the final part of the novel can be read as having both beneficial and negative implications. Hareton acquires the learning and social skills required for union with Cathy; but he also appears to lose power – including sexual power – in his submission to this option. This might be read in terms of a repetition of Catherine's choice earlier in the text, where she trades being true to herself for social privilege.

Study focus: Education and intelligence

Lockwood prides himself on his educational standing, but repeatedly misreads both his environment and his companions. Education in the form of reading, however, dignifies Nelly Dean in her role as **narrator** and lends her social status. Brontë appears to make a distinction between education and intelligence, and prizes intelligence, both in terms of information and in terms of emotional wisdom, far above education.

KEY CONTEXT **A03**

Emily and her sisters were relatively well-educated women, since their father permitted them access to all the books in his library, and they were also able to make use of the Mechanics' Institute Library in Keighley. The significance of letters and books throughout the novel both for the progression of the plot, and the development of character demonstrates the value Emily placed upon the role of education for women.

PROGRESS CHECK

Section One: Check your understanding

These tasks will help you to evaluate your knowledge and skills level in this particular area.

1. List three ways in which inheritance is important to the plot.

2. Is Heathcliff a plausible hero? Make brief notes to support your answer.

3. Is Catherine a weak heroine who needs to be rescued? Set out your argument in bullet points.

4. How does Brontë establish and/or subvert the idea of what it means to be a gentleman? Write your ideas in a two-column table.

5. To what extent does Brontë make her female characters obedient and why is this significant? Make brief notes.

6. Is there such a thing as unselfish love in this novel? Write a paragraph.

7. Consider the representations of sanity and insanity in this novel. Write your ideas in a two-column table.

8. To what extent is Cathy a likeable character? Write a list of relevant points.

9. Make brief notes on the ways in which the characters physically interact with each other (in preparation for a consideration of relationships in Victorian society).

10. Is *Wuthering Heights* a nostalgic novel in the sense that its descriptions of the rural landscape seem to take us back in time? Set out your argument in bullet points.

Section Two: Working towards the exam

Choose one of the following three tasks which require longer, more developed answers:

1. How is power represented in *Wuthering Heights*? Who has it and how well is it used?

2. What does Catherine mean when she tells Nelly 'I *am* Heathcliff'?

3. How is the idea of belonging conveyed in this novel?

A01 PROGRESS BOOSTER

For each Section Two task, read the question carefully, select the key areas you need to address, and plan an essay of six to seven points. Write a first draft, giving yourself an hour to do so. Make sure you include supporting evidence for each point, including quotations.

Progress check (rate your understanding on a level of 1 – low, to 5 – high)	1	2	3	4	5
The key actions, motives and thoughts of major and minor characters in the text					
The different ways you can interpret particular characters' words and actions					
How characterisation is linked to key themes and ideas					
The significance of key themes and ideas within the text					
How some key themes (such as property and education) are linked to context					

GENRE

How a text is constructed, its conventions and patterns, and the way the story is told, can be just as important as what is conveyed. By looking at the possible **genres** *Wuthering Heights* mirrors or draws upon, you can shed light on the novel's particular style and substance.

'A rude and strange production'

Wuthering Heights has been noted for its generic ambiguity. In her preface to the 1850 edition of *Wuthering Heights*, Charlotte Brontë labelled it 'a rude and strange production'. It has been called an 'expanded fairytale' by Elliot Gose (*Imagination Indulg'd*, Montreal, Mcgill, Queens University Press, 1972, p. 59); a 'Romantic incest-story: Heathcliff as brother-lover' by Q. D. Leavis (in Rick Rylance (ed.), *Debating Texts*, 1987, p. 145; see also pp. 24–30) and a 'psychological study' by numerous critics both contemporary with the novel and writing today. As Robert Kiely (*The Romantic Novel in England*, 1972) remarks:

> *Wuthering Heights* is like dream *and* like life *and* like history *and* like other works of literature precisely because Brontë rejects the exclusiveness of these categories. They continually inform and define one another. (p. 236)

And it is perhaps precisely this generic uncertainty that continues to fascinate and intrigue so many readers. We can see how the pleasure of the familiar, provided by the text's realism, is challenged by the subversive power of the genres of fantasy and horror. This means that when we read *Wuthering Heights* the enjoyment of the novel's romantic escapism is counterpointed by the stand it takes against convention. *Wuthering Heights* is a novel which causes us to reassess our conventional wisdom, to (re)consider the prejudices that we take for granted, to take delight in contradiction and **paradox**.

Genre-busting

Wuthering Heights then has famously been considered a generically puzzling book to categorise, something of a genre-buster, combining elements of many different genres. With its confident originality it appears to belong to the tradition of the *roman personnel* (the lived fiction). The relationship between art and life provides the central quest for **biographer-critics**. For example, Brontë's first biographer-critic, A. Mary F. Robinson (*Emily Brontë*, 1883, p. 217), painstakingly traced aspects of Heathcliff's behaviour to aspects of Branwell Brontë, Emily's brother. Biographer-critics saw the task of literary criticism as that of exploring the relationships between fiction and reality. In fact, even Charlotte Brontë's responses to some of the early criticisms of *Wuthering Heights* seem to endorse this kind of critical approach.

Other attempts to categorise the novel have seen it as a **Gothic** novel preoccupied with the fantastic and supernatural; a negotiation of the nineteenth-century **novel of manners**, looking at the relationships between culture and nature; a **Romantic** novel, given its pervading fascination with dreams and the unconscious, and the status it accords the imagination; and a visionary novel, preoccupied with **metaphysical** issues of mystical politics – witness the contrast Emily Brontë draws between conventional religion and the overarching metaphysical truths of love and unconventional perception.

This focus on genres is not without its implications for our reading of the text, or its characters. Our decisions about what sort of novel this is will influence what we expect to see in the characters, plot and setting.

KEY CONTEXT (A03)

Biographer-critics of the nineteenth century believed that the key to understanding the novel lay in drawing parallels between Emily Brontë's life and those of her characters.

KEY INTERPRETATION (A05)

Nancy Armstrong (in Stoneman (ed.), *Wuthering Heights: Contemporary Critical Essays*, 1993) argues that the 'enigmatic' figure of Heathcliff is the result of his crossing between literary genres – the Romantic genres of the early nineteenth century, and early Victorian domestic realism.

The Gothic

The Gothic is a form marked by ghosts and the supernatural. Ghost stories and horror stories have no doubt always been told, but the Gothic, as a literary tradition, is actually relatively modern. Characteristic of this kind of fiction is the stranglehold of the past upon the present. In Gothic fiction emphasis is placed upon setting: often gloomy castles and windswept, bleak landscapes. Images of ruin and decay are also typical.

By the nineteenth century, the Gothic was a popular form, and examples include Mary Shelley's *Frankenstein*, Charlotte Brontë's *Villette*, Jane Austen's *Northanger Abbey* and Wilkie Collins's *The Woman in White*.

As a form, Gothic literature lends itself to psychological realism, combining atmospheric power and the imaginative range of romance. It is an emotionally charged kind of literature, dealing with the uncanny and the ambiguous.

Gothic **narratives** are complex and multi-layered. They are given to excess. Ambivalence and contradiction prevent single meanings from being clearly stated. The Gothic is an aesthetic based on feeling and emotion. It is associated with notions of the **sublime**.

Study focus: Features of the Gothic

A03

Typical features of the Victorian Gothic include gloomy settings such as prisons or ancient houses. Wuthering Heights is described by Lockwood as decorated with 'a quantity of grotesque carving lavished over the front, and especially about the principal door ... a wilderness of crumbling griffins' (Vol. I, Ch. I, p. 4). Later in the novel, the house serves as a prison for Cathy and Nelly Dean. Also popular in the Gothic imagination are ghosts, monsters and sexual fantasy. Catherine's ghost appears to Lockwood, who describes the room he is given to sleep in as 'swarming with ghosts and goblins!' (Vol. I, Ch. III, p. 27). The powerful attraction between Catherine and Heathcliff extends beyond the grave, and sees Heathcliff digging up Catherine's grave to lie with her (Vol. II, Ch. XV, p. 289).

A04 **KEY CONNECTION**

Fred Botting's *Gothic* (The New Critical Idiom, 2013) gives a comprehensive account of the history and characteristics of the form. See also *York Notes Companions: Gothic Literature* (2011) by Sue Chaplin.

A04 **KEY CONNECTION**

The first important instance of the Gothic genre is Horace Walpole's *The Castle of Otranto* (1764). *Wuthering Heights* shares a number of features in common with this early example of the genre: both are set in old buildings full of other people's stories; both make a connection between love and the supernatural; both deal with irresistible passions and the friction of inheritance.

STRUCTURE

Dual narration

Brontë frames her narrative in terms of a dual narration, a technique that was virtually unprecedented when she wrote *Wuthering Heights*. *Wuthering Heights* has a distinct and complex narrative structure, in that it is a story within a story within a story. One character tells the story to another character, who then tells the story to us. We read a story, told by a woman (Brontë), related by a man (Lockwood) who has been told the story by a woman (Nelly Dean).

Brontë's first **narrator**, Lockwood, who tells the **frame narrative**, is demonstrably unreliable: he mistakes social relationships and radically misreads Heathcliff from the beginning. Although Nelly Dean's narrative is somewhat less subject to contradiction and denial, it is nevertheless evidently informed by her own preferences, and from time to time her ulterior motives. We are never under the illusion that Nelly Dean's is a neutral or objective narrative. The novel explicitly resists such consolations and insists upon the responsibilities of all readers and storytellers, as, for example, when Nelly admits that she 'was deceived, completely, as you will hear' (Vol. I, Ch. IV, p. 40) in her assumption that Heathcliff was not vindictive.

Some **feminist analyses** have focused on the fact that Nelly Dean's narrative takes precedence over that of Lockwood, and have seen this as Brontë making an intervention into the male bias of much Victorian literature. Others have read it as a **destabilising** of the conventional authority of the narrative voice. However we choose to read it, it is clear that there is a redistribution of power when Nelly takes up the narrative. For more on this topic, see **Language: The narrators**.

Progress booster: Narrators or actors? A05

In his essay 'The Narrators of *Wuthering Heights*', published in 1957, Carl Woodring argues that Nelly and Lockwood can be read as both narrators and actors in the plot. According to his reading, the narrators are not merely neutral commentators on the action, but active participants in it. This shift of emphasis is a significant one since it focuses not merely on form and structure, but also on character and agency (or action – how characters behave in ways that move the plot of the novel forward). Having such a complex narrative frame raises many questions which are at the heart of how we read literature, and what our expectations about truth and story might be.

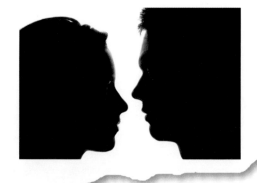

Revision task 6: An unreliable narrator A02

Write about what you have learned about Lockwood as a narrator. Focus on:

● How Lockwood describes the characters around him
● How he relates to his surroundings

LANGUAGE

The narrators

There are two principal narrators in this novel, and this is an important device, which throws into question the authority of the narrator. The aim of the classical narrator, as Frederic Jameson has noted in *The Political Unconscious* (1981), is to restore to the experience of reading some of the pleasure of oral storytelling, which has been to a certain extent lost through the medium of printed books.

That is to say, the conventional narrator confers upon the novel something of the authenticity of a spoken narrative. A narrator makes the story seem 'true' in some sense, just as though we were really in the presence of a person recounting the story to us.

A05

Study focus: Nelly Dean – A revolutionary narrator

The presence of the narrator is comforting, since the narrator is, by virtue of his or her role, a survivor: the narrator must survive to tell the retrospective tale. The voice of the narrator has an authority, which is made even more dramatic in nineteenth-century fiction on account of the fact that nearly all narrators are male. It is doubly significant, therefore, that Emily Brontë chooses two narrators, one male and one female, and that the narrative of Nelly Dean outranks and dispossesses that of Lockwood, the male narrator. Feminist critiques of the novel have focused on this fact and how unusual and revolutionary it must have seemed to Brontë's Victorian readership.

A04 **KEY CONNECTION**

The fairy-tale structure, found in tales like 'Beauty and the Beast', 'Bluebeard' and 'Rumpelstiltskin' permitted women writers to elaborate ideas about choice and love and popular romance within the historical and social context of the marriage contract in the nineteenth century.

Reading between the lines

The construction of two narrators, neither of which is seen to be entirely reliable or impartial, provides for the reader a means of reading what the **post-structuralist** critic Pierre Macherey has called the 'not-said'. By reading 'between the lines' of Nelly's and Lockwood's narratives, the reader is able to interpret information from the text which is never made explicit. In distinguishing between 'reliable' and 'unreliable' accounts, therefore, the reader is able to construct a body of knowledge from which to make judgements about the text, and its characters. As Catherine Belsey points out in *Critical Practice* (1980): 'In *Wuthering Heights* the inadequacies of the perceptions of Lockwood or Nellie [*sic*] Dean do not prevent the reader from seeming to apprehend the real nature of the relationship between Catherine and Heathcliff.' (p. 78)

The fact that we can perceive the accounts given by the narrators as biased and informed by **ideology** permits us to read what the narrators literally *cannot* tell us. An example of this is in Volume I, Chapter II, when Lockwood mistakes the family relationships at Wuthering Heights:

> 'it is strange how custom can mould our tastes and ideas; many could not imagine the existence of happiness in a life of such complete exile from the world as you spend, Mr Heathcliff; yet, I'll venture to say, that, surrounded by your family, and with your amiable lady as the presiding genius over your home and heart –' (Vol. I, Ch. II, p. 13).

Lockwood cannot tell us that his ideological assumptions forbid him to perceive the complex relationship between Heathcliff and Cathy, and yet he is able to alert us to that fact.

Dialect

Emily Brontë's use of the Yorkshire **dialect** has generally been considered to be an accurate account of the accent of the region. In the second edition of the novel, which was edited and amended by Charlotte Brontë, Charlotte changed the way in which Emily had written Joseph's dialect in order to make it more comprehensible. Over time, Charlotte's edition has fallen from favour and most modern editions now take the first edition as their starting point. However, this use of dialect possibly earned *Wuthering Heights* some of its early hostile reviews, since the language and manners of the local characters were criticised for being rough and coarse.

Writing dialect as it sounds is a sensitive issue, since it can make for uncomfortable reading and so make it hard to warm to or understand that character. However, if we take Joseph as an example, his dialect does not serve to make him ridiculous, but rather contributes to our interpretation of his authentic character. We read Joseph as cantankerous, moralising, unyielding and inflexible. His dialect is evidence of his resistance to change and his hostility to strangers. It literally makes him 'difficult to read' or to understand. It thus underlines something in his character. It also emphasises to us that Joseph is proudly himself, unwilling to make that self more palatable to people whose values and world view might differ widely from his own.

Nelly Dean would undoubtedly understand and use this dialect herself, but Brontë's decision to write her speech in standard English serves to emphasise the fact that she is flexible and capable of using and understanding different **discourses** according to her audience. It also suggests that Nelly can manipulate information according to her interests. Thus we can see Brontë's deliberate choice of writing, now in dialect and now in 'heard English', as an expression of character and identity.

Poetic language

The abundance of **metaphor** and **symbol** and the lyricism of the descriptive passages have earned this novel praise for its poetic language:

> One time, however, we were near quarrelling. He said the pleasantest manner of spending a hot July day was lying from morning till evening on a bank of heath in the middle of the moors, with the bees humming dreamily about among the bloom, and the larks singing high up over head, and the blue sky, and bright sun shining steadily and cloudlessly. That was his most perfect idea of heaven's happiness – mine was rocking in a rustling green tree, with a west wind blowing, and bright, white clouds flitting rapidly above; and not only larks, but throstles, and blackbirds, and linnets, and cuckoos pouring out music on every side, and the moors seen at a distance, broken into cool, dusky dells; but close by great swells of long grass undulating in waves to the breeze; and the woods and sounding water, and the whole world awake and wild with joy. He wanted all to lie in an ecstasy of peace; I wanted all to sparkle, and dance in a glorious jubilee. (Vol. II, Ch. X, p. 248)

Brontë's evident delight in the sensual life and the pleasure she takes in language are given full latitude in such passages. Lord David Cecil praises the rhythm of Brontë's prose as 'unfailingly beautiful; a varied, natural, haunting cadence, now buoyantly lilting, now surging like the sea' (*Early Victorian Novelists*, revised edition, 1958, p. 191). In fact, in this novel there are numerous correspondences with Emily Brontë's poetry.

KEY INTERPRETATION

Psychoanalytic theorists such as Jay Clayton (1987) have drawn on the Lacanian view of language (see **Extract analysis: Volume I, Chapter IX**) as alienating, and alienation as a crucial part of what it means to be human, to consider Brontë's use of dialect and language in her novel. The Lacanian view of alienation is closely linked to identity. Because we fail to understand Joseph, we cannot identify with him, and are alienated from him.

Imagery and symbolism

Animal imagery

Brontë frequently uses animal imagery as a metaphor for some human frailty or moral deficiency: Linton, for example, is described as a 'chicken' (Vol. II, Ch. VI, p. 207), Hareton a 'dog' (Vol. II, Ch. XVIII, p. 310), Heathcliff a 'mad dog' (Vol. II, Ch. I, p. 162) and a 'savage beast' (Vol. II, Ch. II, p. 169), Edgar as a 'lamb [who] threatens like a bull' (Vol. I, Ch. XI, p. 114). Lockwood's mistaken apprehension of a heap of dead rabbits as a chairful of cats identifies him not only as unobservant, but also as someone who is incapable of reading animal imagery. Given the preponderance of such imagery in this novel, it is therefore entirely appropriate that his **narratorial** role is quickly taken over by Nelly Dean. The description of the male characters in this novel as beasts can be read as explaining Catherine as a reluctant bride.

As Mark Schorer ('Fiction and the Matrix of Analogy', *Kenyon Review* 11:4, 1949) points out, most of the metaphorical references to animals in *Wuthering Heights* are references to wild animals: 'Hareton's whiskers encroached *bearishly* over his cheeks', and Heathcliff denies the paternity of 'that bear'; Heathcliff is a 'fierce, pitiless, *wolfish* man' (p. 547).

For an unsigned review in the *Christian Remembrancer* in 1857, the recognition that Emily Brontë's 'heroines scratch and tear, and bite, and slap … The men … roll, and grapple, and struggle, and throttle and clutch and tear and trample' was clear evidence of her moral degradation.

Clifton Snider has given a comprehensive account of the animal imagery in this novel, reading such imagery in terms of vampiric **archetypes**. He points out that this is a novel rife with vicious animals: that it is the bite from the Thrushcross Grange guard dog, Skulker, which presents the initial disruption in the childhood relationship between Catherine and Heathcliff, and that Heathcliff himself is described as both supernatural – 'a ghoul, or a vampire' (Vol. II, Ch. XX, p. 330) – and animal – a 'mad dog' (Vol. II, Ch. I, p. 162).

Dreams and ghosts

Dreams are an important key to knowledge in this novel, and the dreams and hallucinatory elements of the text have anticipated twentieth-century **psychoanalytic criticism**.

Dreams demonstrate a way of thinking through the forbidden. They are equipped with a magic all of their own. In the novel, dreams are clearly of central importance and their relation to magic, visions and ghostly apparitions is never understated. Lockwood's dream of the child Cathy begging to be let in is disturbing on two levels. It is grisly, and the gratuitous cruelty of him sawing her wrist against the broken glass is uncomfortable. But as Frank Kermode (*The Classic*, 1975) suggests, it is also disturbing because neither Lockwood nor Heathcliff really believes that it was a dream. It therefore doubly resists any attempts to think about it in rational terms.

The extravagance of the ghostly, the supernatural and the unearthly in this novel is entirely devoted to the relationship between Catherine and Heathcliff, and to descriptions of them as individuals. This achieves its most profound exemplification when Catherine is dying, and Heathcliff is described by Nelly as a 'creature [not] of my own species' (Vol. II, Ch. I, p. 162), and then again towards the end of the novel when she wonders 'Is he a ghoul, or a vampire?' (Vol. II, Ch. XX, p. 330). As Clifton Snider suggests, Brontë's decision to make Heathcliff her hero can be read as an intervention into the Victorian prejudice against outsiders, such as gypsies and beggars, as well as their fascination for and prejudice against the supernatural.

A04 **KEY CONNECTION**

Much of the most potent imagery in *Wuthering Heights* is also to be found in Emily Brontë's poetry. Compare, for example, Heathcliff's tormented account of being unable to sleep for love of Catherine and his desire to be reunited with her dead body, with the poem 'Sleep brings no joy to me' (Emily Brontë, *The Complete Poems*, 1995, p. 55).

A03 **KEY CONTEXT**

In her childhood, Emily Brontë was influenced by the household servants who recounted supernatural tales set in northern England.

Study focus: Nelly's vision

Frank Kermode considers the dreams of the novel in his analysis, paying particular attention to the 'vision' that Nelly has by the signpost of the child Hindley who 'turns into' Hareton, who in turn 'turns into' Heathcliff. He argues that although not strictly a dream this has many similarities with a real dream in terms of its transformations and displacements. The confusion of generations, Hindley, Hareton and Heathcliff mingling and merging, qualifies our sense of their identities and the sense of all **narrative** explanations offered in the text. Because Brontë refuses to offer us any naturalistic explanation of Nelly's experience, it joins the other instances of occult phenomena which are 'only indeterminately related to the natural narrative. And this serves to muddle routine single readings, to confound explanation and expectation, and to make necessary a full recognition of the intrinsic **plurality** of the text' (*The Classic*, 1975, p. 129).

Revision task 7: Dreams and the supernatural A02

Write about the way that dreams and the supernatural give us clues to the main **themes** and plot of the novel while adding greatly to the tension and atmosphere. Focus on:

- Lockwood's dreams when he visits Wuthering Heights
- Catherine's dreams about heaven
- Ghosts

Landscape as a metaphor

Many critics have paid attention to Brontë's use of landscape imagery, and the way in which landscape frequently functions as a **metaphor** for human behaviour or characteristics in this novel. Mark Schorer notes that 'Human conditions are like the activities of the landscape, where rains flood … spirits are at high water mark … illnesses are weathered' ('Fiction and the Matrix of Analogy', 1949, p. 545).

Faces, too, are like landscapes, with countenances regularly clouding over and then brightening. Catherine experiences whole 'seasons of gloom' (Vol. I, Ch. X, p. 92) , and 'her humour was a mere vane for constantly varying caprices' (Vol. II, Ch. I, p. 160).

Progress booster: Landscape and character

It is worth considering what the implications of Brontë's use of landscape are for your understanding of the characters in the novel and their development. We first see the landscape through Lockwood's eyes as difficult to navigate, and hostile, and the first characters he encounters also exhibit these qualities. By the end of the novel, when all the conflicts are resolved, his closing remarks detail the 'benign sky', and the 'quiet earth' (Vol. II, Ch. XX, p. 337). Although by now we know not to trust Lockwood's account entirely, we can nevertheless assume that these two conflicting descriptions of the landscape serve not as pure setting, but as a commentary on the nature and lives of the inhabitants of that landscape.

PROGRESS CHECK

Section One: Check your understanding

These tasks will help you to evaluate your knowledge and skills level in this particular area.

1.   How important is the landscape for establishing this as a **Gothic** novel? Make brief notes.

2.   Note three examples of excessive or macabre imagery in this novel.

3.   How does Brontë establish fear in her novel? Make a list of bullet points.

4.   How does Brontë make use of the **sublime** in her novel? Make a list of examples.

5.   Make brief notes on Nelly's reaction to the power of dreams and visions.

6.   *Wuthering Heights* is a tale within a tale. Make notes on the implications of this for the reader.

7.   What in your opinion is the central mystery of the novel? Make brief notes.

8.   To what extent is the novel structured like a fairy tale? Make a list of your ideas.

9.   How far can the house Wuthering Heights be considered as an example of the traditional castle of Gothic literature? Find evidence to support your answer.

10.   To what extent is the novel structured around social realism? Make brief notes.

Section Two: Working towards the exam

Choose one of the following three tasks which require longer, more developed answers:

1.   How does Brontë use the 'Chinese box' structure of this novel in order to establish suspense? (See page 13.)

2.   Consider the creation of atmosphere with reference to either the house or to landscape in *Wuthering Heights* and *Rebecca*.

3.   How does Brontë make use of poetic language to create effect in *Wuthering Heights*? Compare the novel with three poems from 'Love Poetry Through the Ages'.

 PROGRESS BOOSTER

For each Section Two task, read the question carefully, select the key areas you need to address, and plan an essay of six to seven points. Write a first draft, giving yourself an hour to do so. Make sure you include supporting evidence for each point, including quotations.

Progress check (rate your understanding on a level of 1 – low, to 5 – high)	1	2	3	4	5
How Brontë structures the narrative					
How point of view contributes to characterisation					
How an individual text can modify our understanding of a genre					
The dramatic effect of the landscape					
The use of vocabulary and imagery for poetic effect within a prose narrative					

CONTEXTS

Historical context

Social and economic factors

Emily Brontë's contemporary readers would have been unsurprised by the story of Heathcliff as a foundling from the port of Liverpool: orphans, foundlings and child beggars were a common social problem in the nineteenth century. When families were unable to feed or protect their children, they left them in workhouses and churches in the hope that Christian charity or social justice would look after them. Indeed, Heathcliff's background, tantalisingly obscure as it might seem within the novel, can be read against the social upheavals of Brontë's own time, the key factor in which was the Industrial Revolution.

The effects of the first Industrial Revolution in the late eighteenth century, when the novel is set, were profoundly felt in almost every aspect of daily life. These effects became increasingly tangible through the nineteenth century and would have been well known to early readers of the novel. The mechanisation of industries such as the textile industry meant increased productivity and trade expansion. This in turn saw an enormous shift in the population from rural communities dependent on agriculture, to the towns and cities which swelled in population. The **Romantic** and nostalgic references to nature and the moors as a place of childhood paradise in *Wuthering Heights* might also be read in this context.

Inheritance laws

Key to understanding the plot of *Wuthering Heights* is an appreciation of how the inheritance laws worked in favour of men and against women's interests in the eighteenth century. According to these laws, Cathy cannot inherit Thrushcross Grange when her father, Edgar, dies. Instead, the property automatically passes to Linton as Isabella's son, because males have precedence over females in the inheritance of property. However, should Linton die the property would revert to Cathy, as the sole surviving heir. It is for this reason that Heathcliff is so keen for Cathy and Linton to marry, for once they are married and Cathy is his daughter-in-law, her property automatically becomes his.

Men and women

Inequality between men and women in society extended into every area. It is therefore possible to read *Wuthering Heights* as an extraordinary critique of the social conditions for women, since, as Eva Figes points out in *Sex and Subterfuge: Women Writers in 1850* (1982), Victorian women writers had been largely prevented from writing social or political criticism in their novels owing to their vulnerable position as women writing in a male-dominated cultural milieu. The rural setting of *Wuthering Heights* can be seen as indicative of the position of women as isolated from culture and modern industry, though it also accurately reflects Emily Brontë's own lived experience.

Social upheaval

The historical period during which the novel is based was a time of enormous social upheaval, seeing both the American Revolution, in which thirteen colonies broke away from the British Empire to become the United States of America and rejected the authority of the British Government to govern their territories, and the French Revolution, which had an

KEY CONTEXT **A03**

The Irish potato famine (1845–52), caused by a potato blight, brought thousands of refugees to the port of Liverpool. During the famine more than a million people died in Ireland and another million emigrated. The impact of the blight upon a population almost entirely dependent on the potato for food was extensive. The social realism of finding Heathcliff as an orphan in Liverpool is therefore entirely credible.

enormous impact upon the whole of Europe. It is possible to read Heathcliff as a revolutionary figure, a man not born into social rank but nevertheless contriving to bring down the old establishment of two powerful houses.

Settings

The novel is set in the bleak moorside of Yorkshire, and the geography of the novel can be considered as a character itself. The desolate landscape is difficult to negotiate, and especially given to harsh weather. This acts as a **metaphor** for the uncertain moral landscape which the characters inhabit.

There are various contenders for the 'real' house upon which the **eponymous** house, Wuthering Heights, is believed to be based. One is a Yeoman house called High Sunderland which can be found near Law Hill, the school near Halifax where Emily taught in 1838. Another is a ruined farmhouse known as Top Withens. Similarly, Thrushcross Grange is believed to be based upon an amalgamation of Shibden Hall, also near Halifax, and Ponden Hall near Stanbury. Much as they invoke real houses in their powerful descriptions it must be remembered that these are houses of the imagination. The two locations are **structural oppositions**, in that Wuthering Heights is isolated, dark and forbidding, and set upon the hillside, whereas Thrushcross Grange is more sunny, and located in the valley.

Although the two locations are only four miles apart, the characters frequently miss their way going between the two and the journey from one to the other is considered perilous and fraught. Both sites are representative of a certain social status, and Heathcliff, the outsider, ends up welcome in neither. The bleakly isolated setting and the difficulty of mobility and access are revealing of many of the novel's **themes** of social class, exclusion, property and identity. The descriptions of the setting are in direct contrast with the Romantic view of the open landscape as **sublime** and uplifting.

 **KEY CONTEXT**

A ruined farmhouse known as Top Withens (also Top Withins), which lies on the Pennine Way east of Withins Heights and within walking distance of the parsonage, bears a plaque from the Brontë Society which reads: 'This farmhouse has been associated with Wuthering Heights, the Earnshaw home in Emily Brontë's novel. The buildings, even when complete, bore no resemblance to the house she described, but the situation may have been in her mind when she wrote of the moorland setting of the Heights' (Brontë Society, 1964). This plaque was placed here in response to many enquiries.

Revision task 8: Two different worlds   A02

Wuthering Heights and Thrushcross Grange can be seen to represent two completely different ways of seeing the world. Write about how Brontë presents the two locations. Focus on:

* The differing descriptions of the two houses
* Their contrasting values

Literary context

Emphasis upon a literary context for the novel has been threefold. First, critics have pointed out the poetic qualities of the novel and have cited the influence of Byron (see portrait, right). Indeed, a common critical reading of Heathcliff is to see him as a **Byronic hero**, following a review in *The Examiner* in 1848. (This is an unsigned review, reproduced in Miriam Allott, ed. *The Brontës*, 1974, and Pauline Nester, ed., *Emily Brontë: Wuthering Heights*, 2003.) More sophisticated modern versions of this approach include Gilbert and Gubar's reading in *The Madwoman in the Attic*, where they consider the novel as a revision of the Miltonic myth of the Fall, and Harold Bloom's reading of the novel as a critique of Byron's *Manfred*. Such readings see literature as part of the real life we lead, not just reflective of it, and

argue that the literary texts we create respond to and modify those we have read. The Byronic influences have been particularly discussed by Winifred Gérin in her biography of Emily Brontë.

A second source of influence has been considered to be the **Gothic** genre, and critics have read the significance of ghosts and dreams in this context. *Wuthering Heights* is rich in all the elements typical of the form of the romance. Parallels might be drawn with Mary Shelley's *Frankenstein*, for example, with the **theme** of the divided and monstrous self being played out in the character of Heathcliff. For more on the Gothic, see **Part Four: Genre**.

A third strand of literary influence might be seen to be the effect of fictional realism. According to the Victorian critic Matthew Arnold, realist fiction amounts to a 'criticism of life'. In realist fiction, plots have the fluidity of life and the characters are endowed with psychological, social or natural authenticity. Realist fiction, then, leads people to draw conclusions not just about books but about life in general, and so literature has a moral obligation to be true.

The Brontë family

Following the deaths of their mother and two elder sisters in the 1820s, Charlotte, Emily, Anne and Branwell Brontë were brought up by their father and their aunt in the parsonage at

Haworth and lived relatively remotely from their community, as Charlotte explains in the biographical notice which prefaces most editions of the text of *Wuthering Heights*. Living slightly set apart from the rest of their community, near the churchyard rather than in the terraced houses of Haworth, they took their chief enjoyment from literary compositions which they invented for each other, most famously the sagas of the mythical islands of Gondal which inspired their later poetry. The poetic quality of Emily Brontë's writing in *Wuthering Heights* has been seen as one of the novel's greatest strengths. Anne, Emily and Charlotte are seen in this portrait (left) by Branwell, whose image was painted out.

KEY INTERPRETATION   **A05**

In Mary Shelley's *Frankenstein* (first published in 1818), the scientist Victor Frankenstein brings a body, constructed of different parts, back to life. Heathcliff's desire for Catherine, which extends beyond the grave, can be seen in this context. Gilbert and Gubar (*The Madwoman in the Attic: The Woman Writer and the Nineteenth-Century Literary Imagination*, 1979) famously suggest the possibility of *Wuthering Heights* as a 'deliberate copy' of Mary Shelley's *Frankenstein*.

KEY INTERPRETATION   **A05**

Allan Lloyd Smith's reader *Modern Gothic: A Reader* is a lively collection of essays which considers the Gothic in a variety of forms and will be useful for your understanding of how Brontë's novel has influenced later works.

Comparative texts

Women and society

Central to the action of the novel *Wuthering Heights* is the social choice that Catherine must make regarding marriage. Starkly put, her choice is between a life of convention, security, civil passivity and emotional starvation; and a life of passion, authenticity, insecurity and potential financial and spiritual ruin. Virginia Woolf's novel *Mrs Dalloway* (1925) might also be read as being predicated upon this decision. Clarissa Dalloway, like Catherine, chooses to marry conventionally, though her authentic life is spent imaginatively constructing an alternative life in which she is drawn to the grand themes of love, madness, chaos and death.

The ways in which these two female authors wrote deeply challenged the conventions of novel writing. Brontë's psychological realism can be seen as setting the benchmark for Virginia Woolf's highly original and personalised 'stream-of-consciousness' writing. The radical disconnect between the social lives of their main female characters and their interior lives is profound and destabilising, suggesting that the conventions of society operate to make women ill.

In both novels there is an emphasis upon sensual writing which depicts a life of sensation and poetic engagement with the world. In both cases this emotionally charged **narrative** which underpins and challenges the conventional story of marriage and belonging is figured as the more rewarding life.

Love through the ages

Whether or not we agree that *Wuthering Heights* is primarily a love story, it explores its theme of enduring love in powerful and memorable ways which, although they were deeply challenging to Victorian society, nevertheless thoughtfully engaged with its **discourse** of religion as a redemptive force. The ostensibly transgressive notion that love endures beyond the grave might be seen to be at the heart of Christian values, and the idea that pure, unfettered love supercedes social convention is encapsulated in the Christian doctrine of forgiveness, as Lockwood's puzzling dream of the 'first of the seventy-first' can be seen to suggest.

The idea of love extending beyond the grave can be found in the poetry of Christina Rossetti (below right), most particularly her poem 'Remember', and in Charlotte Mew's poem 'A Quoi Bon Dire', both of which take love after death as their theme. Tony Harrison's poem 'Timer' uses the emblems of someone, in this case a ring, to re-create their physical presence, in a move similar to the ways in which Catherine's diaries evoke her physical presence at the beginning of the novel. 'La Belle Dame Sans Merci' by John Keats (below left) figures a wild, ghostly lover who brings about the ruination of the knight because of her irresistible seductive charms, which might be read as having parallels with the relationship between Catherine and Edgar.

A04 **KEY CONNECTION**

In *Persuasion* (1817), Jane Austen is also alive to the financial and social aspects of the marriage contract, but she is clear that the recipe for a happy marriage includes a deep reciprocal love: mere social compatibility is insufficient.

CRITICAL INTERPRETATIONS

Critical history

Reception and early reviews

A number of early reviews of the novel praised it for its imaginative potency while criticising it for being strange and ambiguous. In a biographical notice attached to many modern versions of the novel, Charlotte Brontë complains that the novel did not receive sufficient merit at its initial reception, but *Wuthering Heights* did not go unrecognised by its early readers. Literary critics repeatedly acknowledged its originality, genius and imaginative power – even if they also complained about its moral ambiguity.

Following Charlotte Brontë's clarification of the gender of Ellis Bell, Victorian readers began to place *Wuthering Heights* in the **Gothic** category, a category of literature peculiarly associated with women. Dante Gabriel Rossetti, in 1854, describes *Wuthering Heights* as:

> a fiend of a book, an incredible monster, combining all the stronger female tendencies from Mrs Browning to Mrs Brownrigg. The action is laid in Hell, – only it seems places and people have no English names there. (Letters of Dante Gabriel Rosetti to William Allingham, 1854–1870)

For the Victorians, *Wuthering Heights* was unarguably an immoral and uncivilised book. It deeply challenged all their ideas about propriety and literature. Equally, by the 1920s it was just as clear that its great value and message was **metaphysical**. Lord David Cecil, Professor of English Literature at Oxford, helped to integrate *Wuthering Heights* into the canon of English Literature in his famous chapter in *Early Victorian Novelists* (1935). He argues that Brontë's motivation in *Wuthering Heights* was an exploration of the meaning of life:

> Her great characters exist in virtue of the reality of their attitude to the universe; they look before us on the simple epic outline which is all that we see of man when revealed against the huge landscape of the cosmic scene (p. 151).

Nineteenth-century views

Following Charlotte's lead, some nineteenth-century analyses of *Wuthering Heights* emphasised the psychological elements of the novel's plot and characters. The critic Sydney Dobell praised Emily Brontë for her portrayal of the 'deep unconscious' truth of Catherine Earnshaw's personality (in E. Jolly (ed.), *The Life and Letters of Sydney Dobell*, vol. 1, 1878, pp. 169–74). However, Dobell insisted that *Wuthering Heights* was not by Emily but was an early work by Charlotte Brontë. According to Dobell, Charlotte Brontë understood that 'certain crimes and sorrows are not so much the result of intrinsic evil as of a false position in the scheme of things'. Dobell's is a view that anticipates some **feminist discussions** of Catherine's decisions and the consequences of those decisions.

Much early criticism tended to look to Emily Brontë's life to understand elements in her work. Such criticism is based on a view that the relationship between literature and the world is relatively straightforward, that reality exists, and that it is literature's job to describe it. The role of literary criticism, according to this view, is to assess the accuracy of the representations, and also to assess the moral content of the work, for literature and the arts in general were held to be an integral part of the civilised life, and thus should contribute to the moral fabric of society.

Twentieth-century views

Close critical attention to Brontë's novel begins with C. P. Sanger ('The Structure of "Wuthering Heights"', 1926) and Lord David Cecil (*Early Victorian Novelists*,1935), both of whom wished to distance criticism from moral judgement and to proceed from an analysis of the formal elements of the text. Cecil's elaboration of the 'storm and calm' structure of *Wuthering Heights* has become one of the most widely accepted of all readings. He argues that the novel is based on a foundation of the dynamic relation between two spiritual principles:

> the principle of storm – of the harsh, the ruthless, the wild, the dynamic; and …
> the principle of calm – of the gentle, the merciful, the passive and the tame …
> in spite of their apparent opposition these principles are not conflicting. (Cecil, *Early Victorian Novelists*, revised edition, 1958, p. 151)

Critics such as Cecil and Sanger prepared the ground for the **new critics** such as Mark Schorer. Schorer was the first to investigate patterns of imagery in *Wuthering Heights*, in 1949. He sees the novel as a moral story about the futility of grand passion. Other new critics include Dorothy Van Ghent, who drew attention to the **metaphors** of windows and thresholds.

Contemporary approaches

Marxist responses

Marxist criticism has seen the novel in terms of its social context, looking for connections between the novel and the political, social and economic conditions under which it was produced.

David Wilson

The first consistent attempt to read *Wuthering Heights* in terms of class oppression and struggle was David Wilson's article 'Emily Brontë: First of the Moderns' (Modern Quarterly Miscellany, No 1, 1947, pp 94–115). Distancing himself from the **biographical** theories of the novel's origins, Wilson dedicates his reading to the project of picturing 'Emily Brontë in a new light, the light of West Riding social history' (p. 94). He provides a detailed history of Haworth and its region, describing the freedom of its independent yeomen in medieval times, both from the feudal system and from the Roman Catholic Church, suggesting that Haworth was a proudly politicised place from its early days. He continues by describing how mechanised industry devastated local hand-loom weavers and gives detailed evidence that 'these social storms were far too near for the sisters to have lived the quiet secluded lives that have been pictured' (p. 96).

A04 **KEY CONNECTION**

There have been many film versions of the novel, the earliest of which was A. V. Bramble's 1920 silent film.

A05 **KEY INTERPRETATION**

Wilson's purpose in such a reading is to account for the real social conditions in which a book like *Wuthering Heights* was produced, seeing it neither as the product of isolated genius nor as the muddled ramblings of a social recluse. For a confirmation of the effect of the Industrial Revolution on Haworth, see Juliet Barker's biography of the Brontës (1994).

Terry Eagleton

Perhaps the most famous **Marxist analysis** of the novel is given by Terry Eagleton in *Myths of Power: A Marxist Study of the Brontës* (1975), in which he considers the novel in terms of its reference to class, economics and history. Eagleton is interested in the novel's relationship to Victorian **ideology**, looking at how that ideology is both reflected and produced by the novel.

Wuthering Heights is ideological, argues Eagleton, because it presents a 'world-view' – it represents conflicts without being fragmented by conflict itself. Contradictions and oppositions coexist in this novel in a profound but not unsatisfying tension.

The primary contradiction that Eagleton explores in relation to this assertion is the choice that Catherine must make between Edgar Linton and Heathcliff. He identifies that choice as the pivotal event of the novel and the precipitating factor in all the tragic events that follow. Catherine chooses Edgar Linton because of his social superiority, which Eagleton identifies as an act of 'bad faith', and she is, he judges, rightly criticised by Heathcliff for this betrayal of their more authentic love. The social self, Eagleton argues, is shown to be false not because it is simulated or a lie, but because it exists in a contradictory and negative relationship to authentic selfhood, which is shown in Catherine's love of Heathcliff.

Eagleton's essay also analyses Heathcliff's position in the novel in terms of his place in the family structure, local society and the economic system of rural Yorkshire at the turn of the century. Because Heathcliff is spirited out of nowhere into this family, he has no social or domestic status and he is therefore both a threat to the established order and an opportunity for it to be reinvented. Heathcliff disturbs the establishment because he has no legitimate place in its system. Eagleton's analysis turns on the issue of liberty and oppression. The fact that there is no opportunity for freedom either within or outside the system is a consequence of bourgeois society.

Heathcliff learns to see culture as a means of oppression, and he acquires it to use as a weapon. This association of culture with violence is further played out in the novel in the ferocity which is used to defend property, from the moment that Catherine is savaged by Skulker, the Linton's bulldog, to the complex seizure of property by Heathcliff in the second part of the novel.

Raymond Williams

Two years before Eagleton's *Myths of Power*, the Marxist critic Raymond Williams had published an insightful reading of *Wuthering Heights* in his book *The Country and the City* (1973), accounting for the relationship between Catherine and Heathcliff in terms of alienation rather than oppression. Although Williams acknowledges that it is class and property that divide Heathcliff and Catherine, he argues that the solution to their division is never conceived in terms of social reform. What Brontë privileges above all, he argues, is human intensity and a profound connection between people:

> The tragic separation between human intensity and any available social settlement is accepted from the beginning in the whole design and idiom of the novel. The ... plot is ... sustained by a single feeling, which is the act of transcendence. (p. 176)

This concept of **transcendence** as a response to alienation from social possibilities is also important in Eagleton's reading.

Progress booster: Heathcliff's contradiction

A05

You should analyse Heathcliff's character from a range of different viewpoints, bringing to bear different critical positions and drawing your own conclusions. In social terms the Heights can be read as embodying the world of the gentleman farmer – the petty-bourgeois yeoman – whereas the Grange epitomises the gentry. Eagleton argues that Heathcliff's social relation to both the Heights and the Grange is one of the most complex issues in the novel. Heathcliff fiercely highlights the contradictions between the two worlds in opposing the Grange and undermining the Heights. He embodies a passionate human protest against the marriage market values of both the Heights and the Grange, while violently caricaturing precisely those values in his calculatedly callous marriage to Isabella. In this, Heathcliff can be seen to be a parody of capitalist activity, yet he is not simply this, for he is also a product of and participant in that system. The contradiction of the novel is that Heathcliff both embodies and antagonises the values that he wishes to contest.

The ending of the novel, with its ostensible integration of the values of the two worlds, might seem to weaken Eagleton's argument that the contradictions of the novel coexist in an exciting and productive tension. However, he argues that this conclusion depends upon how one reads Hareton Earnshaw. If Hareton is read as a surrogate and diluted Heathcliff, then the novel's ending does indeed suggest a reconciliation between the gentry and the capitalist. If, however, Hareton is read as a literal survivor of yeoman stock, then what effectively happens is that he is entirely conquered by the **hegemony** or authority of the Grange.

A03 **KEY CONTEXT**

Because Marxists see ideology as what makes people choose to cooperate with, endorse and naturalise the class structure, they are particularly interested in the contradictions which arise at boundaries between classes and other social groups. To Marxists these contradictions reveal ideology for what it is: an imposed set of beliefs, and not the 'natural order' of things, or inevitable.

Feminist responses

Sandra Gilbert and Susan Gubar

Feminist criticism has seen the novel in terms of its language, and in terms of the strategies and opportunities that are open to women in the novel. Feminist and gender criticism has also provided some interesting readings of the ambivalent representations of gender in *Wuthering Heights*, not least of which is Gilbert and Gubar's reading of Heathcliff as 'female' in the sense that second sons, bastards and daughters are female. Heathcliff is 'female' because he is dispossessed of social power. He has no status, no social place and no property. For the majority of the novel, he is only Heathcliff, never Mr Heathcliff, or the Master, in contrast to Edgar Linton. Heathcliff's rebellions against the social conventions of class, marriage and inheritance similarly suggest that he can be read as 'female' since endorsing such conventions only serves the interests of patriarchal culture.

This reading of Heathcliff as female seems to go against the grain of conventional critical agreement that he epitomises heroic masculinity, especially when compared with the fair, slim, soft Edgar. But when these characters are read in terms of their social power, Heathcliff has no social position, and Edgar is always referred to as 'the Master'. Edgar, who is most at home in the library, has all the power of masculine culture behind him. His mastery is contained in documents, books, rent-rolls, patriarchal domination. Edgar is the guardian of culture. Heathcliff is feminine in the sense that he is unpropertied, dispossessed, subject to the rule of the father, an outcast.

A05 **KEY INTERPRETATION**

When Heathcliff is referred to as 'Mr Heathcliff' by Lockwood (Vol. I, Ch. II, p. 13), this is instructive for it reveals that Lockwood's relationship with Heathcliff is as misguided as many of his other assumptions.

In *The Madwoman in the Attic*, Gilbert and Gubar interrogate *Wuthering Heights* in terms of what they term 'feminist mythologies'. They see the project of the novel as rewriting and revising the Miltonic myth of the Fall. They also identify the novel as a distinctively nineteenth-century response to the problems of origins, and as an exploration into the nature of heaven and hell.

In their reading of the novel in terms of writing against the male tradition, Gilbert and Gubar see *Wuthering Heights* as a 'Bible of Hell', a novel which values the natural over the cultural, the anarchic over the world of organised repression. Wuthering Heights, the house of the title, is hellish by conventional standards, but for Catherine and Heathcliff it represents the kind of non-hierarchical social space in which they are permitted a degree of power which would be denied them elsewhere, since she is female and he is illegitimate, and they are both thereby excluded from power in the conventional world. Thrushcross Grange, across the moor, home of the Linton family and inspired by Shibden Hall in West Yorkshire, represents the standards of patriarchal culture which will be triumphant by the end of the story, but which the novel itself, through its sympathies for Catherine and Heathcliff, implicitly attacks.

Naomi Jacobs

Other feminist critics also make connections between the form of the novel and the historical position of women. Naomi Jacobs, in 'Gender and Layered Narrative in *Wuthering Heights* and *The Tenant of Wildfell Hall*' (1986, reprinted in Patricia Ingham, ed. *The Brontës*, Longman Critical Reader, 2014 first published 2003), gives a legal-social dimension to the question of the **narrative frame**, suggesting that the process of exposing the real constraints of women's lives indicates at least a partial loosening of those constraints. The argument is that Emily Brontë's challenging of the formal authoritative **discourses** of Victorian life itself represents a radical intervention into those structures. She proceeds to document the prevalence of nineteenth-century wife abuse and the reluctance of reviewers to acknowledge its existence. Jacobs then argues that the narrative structure of the novel represents an authorial strategy for dealing with the unacceptability of the subject matter.

Study focus: Identity and mirroring   A05

Focusing on the issue of naming in the novel, Gilbert and Gubar suggest that the writing of the name 'Catherine' in its various manifestations, which Lockwood encounters inscribed into the windowsill, reveals the crucial lack of identity that is common to all women under patriarchy: 'What Catherine, or any girl must learn is that she does not know her own name, and therefore cannot know who she is or whom she is destined to be' (p. 276).

However, as Gilbert and Gubar point out, although Heathcliff can be read as Catherine's other self, he is not her identical double. This was a point first made by Leo Bersani in his book *A Future for Astyanax*. Not only is he male and she female, but he is a survivor, and a usurper of power, while she is a mournful, outcast, ghost. Nevertheless, his fate at the end of the novel mirrors hers: he is unable to eat; he is feverish, and obsessed by the elements; and his death is partly a result of his encounter with culture, in the form of Cathy, who as Edgar Linton's daughter embodies the intervention of patriarchy. And in death, Heathcliff has arranged that his body shall merge with Catherine's until they are indistinguishable.

Deconstructive responses

J. Hillis Miller has provided an influential deconstructive reading of the novel. **Deconstruction** offers an alternative to traditional scholarship that is both playful and challenging. Unwilling to privilege a certain kind of reading, deconstructive criticism argues that there is no one right way to read a text, and that literature does not contain the kinds of unified and universal truths that traditional criticism seeks. Instead, deconstructive criticism considers the way in which all **transcendent** truths, including those judgements we might make about the aesthetic unity of the text, and the inherent truth of the narrative, undo themselves in internal contradictions and incompatibilities. Hillis Miller's reading focuses upon the ways in which the novel resists rational explanation, for example through its structure, language and use of narrators.

'Structure' is a complex term which can be used to refer to many different features of a text. The aspect of *Wuthering Heights* which has generated the most persistent debate is what might be termed its 'narrative structure': namely, the allocation of different parts of the story to different voices, rather than the more conventional narrative form in which one narrator tells his or her story.

C. P. Sanger was among the first critics to argue that the structure of *Wuthering Heights* does in fact conform to a logical strictness and exactitude with regard to its dates. He also argues that the most obvious thing about the structure of the story is the symmetry of the family pedigree: for Sanger, the whole intricate structure 'demonstrates the vividness of the author's imagination' ('The Structure of "Wuthering Heights"', 1926, p. 20).

Psychoanalytic responses

Psychoanalytic readings of *Wuthering Heights* have offered some very rich insights into the novel. Several Victorian critics, perhaps most famously Sydney Dobell (1850), saw the exciting possibilites of considering the text as a study in abnormal psychology. Freudian psychoanalytic theory has offered critics a more precise vocabulary and a more robust explanation for the obsessive and divided mentalities we see in Heathcliff and Catherine.

Because of its nature, the unconscious is normally inaccessible to the conscious mind. Therefore we must pay attention to the secret ways in which it might reveal itself. One of these ways is through dreams, and one of Freud's earliest published works was *The Interpretation of Dreams* (1900). With its emphasis upon dreams that disrupt the smooth flowing of the narrative, and which are hard to assimilate into the main body of the text, *Wuthering Heights* has proved rich territory for dream interpretation, with Lockwood's dreams in Volume I, Chapter III, providing clues to both the plot and the emotions of the characters.

Many modern psychoanalytical studies of *Wuthering Heights* derive not from Freud but from the theories of Jacques Lacan, whose ideas have been of particular interest to literary critics because of their focus on language. Philip K. Wion has made great use of Lacan's theories about language and about the relationship between the child and the mother in his readings of *Wuthering Heights* (see **Extended commentary: Volume I, Chapter IX**). Wion presents the absence of mothers as a key feature of *Wuthering Heights*, which, he argues, can be attributed to the fact that Emily Brontë's mother died when she was three years old. Lacan suggests that the loss of the mother is an essential part of the human condition, and it can be argued that this makes the novel deeply relevant to all who read it.

A03 **KEY CONTEXT**

Victorian reviewers criticised the novel for its confusing structure since it contradicted their belief that it was the novelist's duty to make his or her meaning plain. The multitude of conflicting voices in this novel serves to disturb any such notions of clear and stable meanings.

A04 **KEY CONNECTION**

Northern Ballet regularly tour Claude-Michel Schönberg's 2002 adaptation of *Wuthering Heights* as a ballet. The fact that this enigmatic novel lends itself to such diverse interpretations with such moving and powerful results is testament to the potency of the original story, and its continuing importance for readers today.

KEY INTERPRETATION A05

Claire Colebrook's book *New Literary Histories* (1997) offers a clear and interesting account of new historicist readings of *Wuthering Heights*.

New historicist responses

Recent criticism of *Wuthering Heights* has often favoured **new historicist** approaches to scholarship. These approaches seek to situate the novel in its historical context and argue that works of fiction are not produced in a vacuum, but are informed by the author's and the reader's distinct social, political and cultural environment. Published in 1847, *Wuthering Heights* was written during a period of immense historical upheaval. The Reform Act on women's suffrage had been passed in 1832; Chartism, a working class movement for political reform, was at its height; the great Irish famine, arising from the potato blight, meant that thousands of starving Irish migrants arrived in Liverpool and gave rise to the Young Ireland Movement of the 1840s which campaigned for the dissolution of the Union and advocated Irish independence. An historicist approach to *Wuthering Heights* would argue that the novel is structured around similar anti-hierarchical concerns as those of these political movements.

According to such readings, *Wuthering Heights* is subversive, in that its un-landed characters refuse to remain subservient. The dominant modes of power as exemplified in the characters of Lockwood and the Lintons are thoroughly challenged; traditional gender roles and characteristics are overturned and disparaged; and the novel can be read as a rebellion against traditional values and social mores. As a house, Wuthering Heights is the place where servants disregard the orders of their masters, disenfranchised orphans operate to inherit the land and women defy social expectations of being gracious or playing hostess.

KEY CONNECTION A04

In 2016 a new British adaptation of the novel as a musical was performed at the Iris Theatre in Covent Garden, London. *Wuthering Heights The Musical*, written by Catherine McDonald, gained a four-star review from Mathew Partridge on remotegoat.com.

Clearly, historicist responses to the novel have much in common with **Marxist** and **feminist readings** of the novel. However, unlike Marxist and feminist readings, an historicist approach goes further and argues the novel is itself part of the modes of production that give rise to our understanding, that is the novel does not just reflect history, it produces it. The novel is itself an agent of change. So a novel is not just an example, reflecting a given historical moment, it also functions to operate within that moment, producing and challenging its conditions.

Another aspect of the new historicist approach is to look to the generally overlooked: historical documents and **anecdotes**, sermons and letters of the period. Clearly there is much in *Wuthering Heights* that lends itself to this approach as its structure relies on such overlooked and mildewed texts: the sermon of Jabes Branderham; Catherine's childhood diaries; personal letters either preserved or discovered.

PROGRESS CHECK

Section One: Check your understanding

These tasks will help you to evaluate your knowledge and skills level in this particular area.

1. List three social factors that influence character or plot in *Wuthering Heights*.

2. What elements of the text might a feminist reading of *Wuthering Heights* emphasise? List six points.

3. To what extent is Heathcliff a **Byronic hero**? Make brief notes on the typical qualities of a Byronic hero.

4. Make a list of the key features of the **Gothic** novel and suggestions for how *Wuthering Heights* fits the description.

5. Make brief notes on how a Marxist perspective might discuss power in *Wuthering Heights*.

6. Make a table showing four points of connection between *Wuthering Heights* and another novel you have studied.

7. List four ways in which the setting of the novel reacts to or forms part of the **Romantic** tradition.

8. Make a mind-map showing how Brontë's idea of love extending beyond the grave has its resonances in at least three of the poems you have studied.

9. For the more conservative Victorians *Wuthering Heights* was a deeply immoral book. List five ways in which Brontë challenges the idea of conventional morality.

10. List four elements that a **psychoanalytical reading** of this novel might focus upon.

Section Two: Working towards the exam

Choose one of the following three tasks which require longer, more developed answers:

1. Discuss the **theme** of love enduring beyond death in reference to *Wuthering Heights* and the poems from 'Love Poetry Through the Ages' and demonstrate the relationship between the texts.

2. Is *Wuthering Heights* a moral novel? Compare Brontë's presentation of morality with Ian McEwan's in *Atonement*.

3. In your opinion, how far is *Wuthering Heights* a trangressive text?

A01 PROGRESS BOOSTER

For each Section Two task, read the question carefully, select the key areas you need to address, and plan an essay of six to seven points. Write a first draft, giving yourself an hour to do so. Make sure you include supporting evidence for each point, including quotations.

Progress check (rate your understanding on a level of 1 – low, to 5 – high)	1	2	3	4	5
How some knowledge of context enhances interpretation of the novel					
The different ways the novel can be read, according to critical approaches such as Marxist or feminist					
How comparison with another literary work can deepen understanding of both					
How a reader's interpretation may differ from the author's intended meaning					
How *Wuthering Heights* may be read as a historical document					

ASSESSMENT FOCUS

How will you be assessed?

Each particular exam board and exam paper will be slightly different, so make sure you check with your teacher exactly which Assessment Objectives you need to focus on. You are likely to get more marks for Assessment Objectives 1, 2 and 3 if you are studying AQA/A, but this does not mean you should discount 4 or 5. Bear in mind that if you are doing AS Level, although the weightings are the same, there will be no coursework element.

What do the AOs actually mean?

	Assessment Objective	Meaning
AO1	Articulate informed, personal and creative responses to literary texts, using associated concepts and terminology, and coherent, accurate written expression.	You write about texts in accurate, clear and precise ways so that what you have to say is clear to the marker. You use literary terms (e.g. '**protagonist**') or refer to concepts (e.g. 'the uncanny' or '**archetypes**') in relevant places. You do not simply repeat what you have read or been told, but express your own ideas based on in-depth knowledge of the text and related issues.
AO2	Analyse ways in which meanings are shaped in literary texts.	You are able to explain in detail how the specific techniques and methods used by Brontë to create the text (e.g. **narrative** voice, dialogue, **metaphor**) influence and affect the reader's response.
AO3	Demonstrate understanding of the significance and influence of the contexts in which literary texts are written and received.	You can explain how the text might reflect the social, historical, political or personal backgrounds of Brontë or the time when it was written. You also consider how *Wuthering Heights* might have been received differently over time.
AO4	Explore connections across literary texts.	You are able to explain links between *Wuthering Heights* and other texts, perhaps of a similar **genre**, or with similar concerns, or viewed from a similar perspective (e.g. **feminist**).
AO5	Explore literary texts informed by different interpretations.*	You understand how *Wuthering Heights* can be viewed in different ways, and are able to write about these debates, forming your own opinion. For example, how one critic might view *Wuthering Heights* as a socially realistic exploration of the terrors that civilisation is designed to suppress, whereas another critic might view it as the greatest love story of all time.

* AO5 is not assessed by Edexcel in relation to *Wuthering Heights*.

What does this mean for your revision?

Whether you are following an AS or A Level course, use the right-hand column above to measure how confidently you can address these objectives. Then focus your revision on those aspects you feel need most attention. Remember, throughout these Notes, the AOs are highlighted, so you can flick through and check them in that way.

Next, use the tables on page 97. These help you to understand the differences between a satisfactory and an outstanding response.

Then use the guidance from page 98 onwards to help you address the key AOs, for example how to shape and plan your writing.

Features of **mid-level** responses: the following examples relate to issues of social class in the novel.

	Features	Examples
A01	You use critical vocabulary appropriately for most of the time, and your arguments are relevant to the task, ordered sensibly, with clear expression. You show detailed knowledge of the text.	*'Wuthering Heights' is a novel of great conflicts. One of the ways in which we see these is through the ways in which the characters speak. For example Lockwood speaks more intelligently than Joseph, and they cannot understand each other's worlds. Although Lockwood is more clearly understood, he himself does not understand things for example, when he mistakes the dead rabbits for cats.*
A02	You show straightforward understanding of the writer's methods, such as how form, structure and language shape meanings.	*How we understand the two different narratives depends on how we view the characters. Brontë's representation of Nelly as no-nonsense makes us think that her story is reliable. Because of this we tend to take Nelly's judgements about the other characters as being reliable and so risk missing important clues about them.*
A03	You can write about a range of contextual factors and make some relevant links between these and the task or text.	*The idea of what is **properly feminine**, as in 'the lady', is also explored. When as a child Catherine stays at Thrushcross Grange to recover, she returns to the Heights 'like a lady', not as a grown woman, but as a member of a **higher social class**.*
A04	You consider straightforward connections between texts and write about them clearly and relevantly to the task.	*A **key theme** of the novel is the **tension between true love and marriage**. Brontë is outspoken about the choices available to women. Khaled Hosseini's 'A Thousand Splendid Suns' also focuses on this distinction between marriage as a social institution and the hope of the women characters to find true love.*
A05	You tackle the debate in the task in a clear, logical way, showing your understanding of different interpretations.	*Most people reading 'Wuthering Heights' take a view on the role of **ghosts** in the novel. Some critics have suggested that the novel is not a typical **Gothic** novel. Although the novel does not make simple distinctions between good and evil, superstition and religion, it still has lots of features of the traditional Gothic romance.*

Features of a **high-level** response: these examples relate to a task on narrative perspectives.

	Features	Examples
A01	You are perceptive, and assured in your argument in relation to the task. You make fluent, confident use of literary concepts and terminology; and express yourself confidently.	*Brontë structures her novel through a series of shifting **narratorial** voices. This is a **device** which urges us to question our ideas about the **truth of the story** being told. We are constantly reminded that these accounts are partisan, contradictory and open to revision.*
A02	You explore and analyse key aspects of the writer's use of form, structure and language and evaluate perceptively how they shape meanings.	*Brontë's presentation of Nelly's practical good humour and confidential tone encourages us to see her story as **credible and reliable**. How we approach Nelly therefore prompts us to form **judgements** about the other characters, risking missing other important **textual signals**.*
A03	You show deep, detailed and relevant understanding of how contextual factors link to the text or task.	*In evaluating the **arrival** of **Heathcliff** and his rise to **power** within the novel it can be argued that 'Wuthering Heights' is deeply concerned with issues of **class and social mobility**. Published in 1848, it was written in a time of the emergence of Trade Unionism and the democratic movement of **Chartism**.*
A04	You show a detailed and perceptive understanding of issues raised through connections between texts. You have a range of excellent supportive references.	*Some critics have looked to 'Wuthering Heights' to consider anxieties around the **repression** and **expression** of **sexual passion, violence and desire**. Virginia Woolf's novel 'Mrs Dalloway' also grapples with these issues, but where Brontë's characters demonstrate intense reactions to their unfulfilled desires, Clarissa Dalloway suffers from an inability to resist the **constraints of patriarchy** and the **fragmentations of the self** that living under its conditions imposes.*
A05	You are able to use your knowledge of critical debates, and the possible perspectives on an issue to write fluently and confidently about how the text might be interpreted.	*The impact of **marriage** upon a woman's life is at the heart of the choices that the female characters make in this novel. Isabella could be viewed as lacking complexity, and socially naive. **Feminist theory** has seen her as **'objectified'**, reduced to an agent of her husband's revenge. Her smashing of her wedding ring is a metaphor for her desire to violate her marriage.*

HOW TO WRITE HIGH-QUALITY RESPONSES

The quality of your writing – how you express your ideas – is vital for getting a higher grade, and **AO1** and **AO2** are specifically about **how** you respond.

Five key areas

The quality of your responses can be broken down into **five** key areas.

1. The structure of your answer/essay

- First, get **straight to the point in your opening paragraph**. Use a sharp, direct first sentence that deals with a key aspect and then follow up with evidence or detailed reference.
- **Put forward an argument or point of view** (you won't **always** be able to challenge or take issue with the essay question, but generally, where you can, you are more likely to write in an interesting way).
- **Signpost your ideas** with connectives and references which help the essay flow. Aim to present an overall argument or conceptual response to the task, not a series of unconnected points.
- **Don't repeat points already made,** not even in the conclusion, unless you have something new to add.

Aiming high: Effective opening paragraphs

Let's imagine that you have been asked about what is hidden and what is revealed in *Wuthering Heights*, and the structural and **symbolic** importance of hiding places, graves and bedrooms. Here's an example of a successful opening paragraph:

Gets straight to the point

Good use of quotation

Sets up some interesting ideas that will be tackled in subsequent paragraphs

How comfortable we are as readers with unlocking secrets will determine how we respond to this novel, with its many different layers of interlocking stories. The structure of the novel might seem at first to be deliberately obstructive. It opens with Lockwood's narrative, through which, via a series of barriers: a closed gate, a 'range of gaunt thorns' and an almost impenetrable 'penetralium' we enter Wuthering Heights and the world of the novel. Lockwood's account then gives way to Nelly Dean's. Nelly offers us images of further enclosure: the two houses, the closet bed (which resembles a coffin), the barred door, the soldered casement window. From the beginning of the novel then, we are aware that this will be a novel full of withheld secrets.

2. Use of titles, names, etc.

This is a simple, but important, tip to stay on the right side of the examiners.

- Make sure that you spell correctly the titles of the texts, chapters, authors and so on. Present them correctly too, with inverted commas and capitals as appropriate. For example, 'Wuthering Heights'.
- Use the **full title**, unless there is a good reason not to (e.g. it's very long).
- Use the term 'text' rather than 'book' or 'story'. If you use the word 'story', the examiner may think you mean the plot/action rather than the 'text' as a whole.

3. Effective quotations

Do not 'bolt on' quotations to the points you make. You will get some marks for including them, but examiners will not find your writing very fluent.

The best quotations are:

* Relevant and not too long (you are going to have to memorise them, so that will help you select shorter ones)
* Integrated into your argument/sentence
* Linked to effect and implications

Aiming high: Effective use of quotations

Here is an example of an effective use of a quotation about passion as a source of pain in the novel:

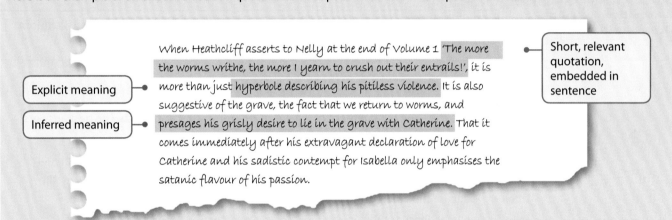

Explicit meaning

Inferred meaning

When Heathcliff asserts to Nelly at the end of Volume 1 'The more the worms writhe, the more I yearn to crush out their entrails!', it is more than just hyperbole describing his pitiless violence. It is also suggestive of the grave, the fact that we return to worms, and presages his grisly desire to lie in the grave with Catherine. That it comes immediately after his extravagant declaration of love for Catherine and his sadistic contempt for Isabella only emphasises the satanic flavour of his passion.

Short, relevant quotation, embedded in sentence

Remember – quotations can also be one or two single words or phrases embedded in a sentence to build a picture or explanation, or they can be longer ones that are explored and picked apart.

4. Techniques and terminology

Mention literary terms, techniques, conventions, critical theories or people **but** make sure that you:

* Understand what they mean
* Are able to link them to what you're saying
* Spell them correctly

5. General writing skills

Try to use standard English as this will mean that your argument sounds authoritative.

* Avoid colloquial or everyday expressions such as 'got', 'alright', 'ok' and so on.
* Use terms such as 'convey', 'suggest', 'imply', 'infer' to explain the writer's methods.
* Refer to 'we' when discussing the audience/reader.
* Avoid assertions and generalisations; don't just state a general point of view, but analyse closely with clear evidence and textual detail.

Note the professional approach here in the choice of vocabulary and awareness of the effect on the reader:

Brontë conveys the sense of a society in conflict with its own past, and mistrustful of its future. She uses the Gothic conventions to challenge the ideas of the time. As readers we too feel haunted by Lockwood's dream as the ghosts of passion and chaos threaten to disrupt our understanding of what is real.

> **EXAMINER'S TIP**
>
> Something examiners pick up is that students confuse **'narrator'** and 'author'. Remember that Lockwood is a character as well as a narrator and don't confuse him with the novel's author, Emily Brontë.

COMPARING *WUTHERING HEIGHTS* WITH OTHER NOVELS

As part of your assessment, you may have to compare *Wuthering Heights* with or link it to other novels you have studied.

Linking or comparison questions might relate to a particular **theme** or idea, for example with a general question as follows:

> **Compare the ways in which the writers of your two chosen texts present the struggle for identity in relationships. You must relate your discussion to relevant contextual factors.**

Or, with a statement to which you have to respond:

> **'Emotional intensity destroys relationships.' By comparing two prose texts, explore the extent to which you agree with this statement.**

You will need to:

Evaluate the issue or statement and have an **open-minded approach**. The best answers suggest meaning**s** and interpretation**s** (plural):

* For example, in relation to the first question: do you agree that the struggle for identity is a key factor in relationships in *Wuthering Heights* and your second novel? Why? How?
* What are the different ways that this question or aspect can be read or viewed?
* What evidence is there in each text for this perspective? How can you present it in a thoughtful, reflective way?
* What are the points of similarity and difference?

Express **original or creative approaches** fluently:

* This isn't about coming up with entirely new ideas, but you need to show that you're actively engaged with thinking about the question, not just reeling off things you have learned.
* **Synthesise** your ideas – pull ideas and points together to create something fresh.
* This is a linking/comparison response, so ensure that you guide your reader through your ideas logically, clearly and with professional language.

Know *what* to compare/contrast: the writer's methods – **form**, **structure** and **language** – will **always** be central to your response. Consider:

* The authorial perspective or voice (who is speaking/writing), standard versus more conventional **narration** (use of flashback, foreshadowing, disrupted time or narrative voice which leads to dislocation or difficulty in reading)
* Different characteristic use of language (lengths of sentences, formal/informal style, **dialect**, accent, balance of dialogue and narration)
* Variety of symbols, images, motifs (how they represent concerns of author/time; what they are and how and where they appear; how they link to critical perspectives; their purposes, effects and impact on the narration)
* Shared or differing approaches (to what extent do Brontë and the author/s of your second text conform to/challenge/subvert approaches to writing about these aspects?)

Writing your response

> **Compare the ways in which the writers of your two chosen texts present the struggle for identity in relationships. You must relate your discussion to relevant contextual factors.**

Introduction to your response

- Discuss quickly what 'struggle for identity' means, and how this applies to both texts.
- Mention the key relationships that exist in *Wuthering Heights* and in the second text.
- You could begin with a powerful quotation to launch into your response. For example:

'Whatever our souls are made of, his and mine are the same; and Linton's is as different as a moonbeam from lightning, or frost from fire.' Catherine tells Nelly in Volume I, Chapter IX of 'Wuthering Heights', comparing her relationship with Heathcliff to that with Edgar. The quotation exemplifies the use of nature to describe human difference, and also the overarching assertion that Heathcliff and Catherine are as one.

Main body of your response

- **Point 1**: start with one particular character's struggle for identity in *Wuthering Heights*: for example, Catherine's battle to define herself in terms of her relationships with Edgar and Heathcliff; how Brontë situates her characters in terms of the issues of the time; why this was/was not 'interesting' for readers at the time, and readers now.
- **Point 2**: now consider a new factor comparing Catherine's struggle with that of another character in Text 2. For example, *In 'Mrs Dalloway' Virginia Woolf suggests that Clarissa's search for identity is refined by her relationships with the other characters, and that the parties she organises are in themselves a form of self-creation, close to a 'religious ceremony'.* How is the struggle in Text 2 presented **differently or similarly** by the writer according to language, form, structures used; and why?
- **Points 3, 4, 5, etc.**: address a range of other factors and aspects, for example other 'struggles for identity' **either** within *Wuthering Heights* **or** in both *Wuthering Heights* and the second text. In what different ways do you respond to these (with more empathy, greater criticism, less interest) – and why? For example:

Catherine's attachment to Heathcliff is so emotionally intense that she hardly distinguishes between her self and his. This contrasts with her marriage to Edgar which, though loving, is less charged. Catherine's inability to reconcile these two loves leads to her illness. Edgar's appeal for Catherine is not only his wealth, but also his refinement, and his care for her. When they first meet, Catherine is injured and Edgar's family offers her a new version of herself. She returns to her old life 'like a lady', which Brontë suggests throws her true sense of self into disarray. Brontë requires us to decide whether Catherine's feelings for Edgar represent self-denial or a survival strategy.

Conclusion

- Synthesise elements of what you have said into a final paragraph that leaves the examiner believing that you have engaged with the set task and the texts.

In 'Mrs Dalloway' Clarissa has a sense of herself in society and in her marriage as being 'invisible; unseen; unknown'. In 'Wuthering Heights' Catherine describes her marriage to Edgar as rendering her 'an exile, and outcast, thenceforth, from what had been my world.' Both texts imply that true identity is realised in an authentic, passionate relationship but that such relationships are impossible in civilised society, which seeks to constrain them and redefine women within the parameters of social propriety. The authors suggest that this can lead to a sense of self-annihilation, and even a descent into madness and death.

COMPARING *WUTHERING HEIGHTS* WITH POETRY

Depending on the course you are following, you may have to compare aspects of *Wuthering Heights* with at least two poems from the Anthology you are studying.

A typical question in this case would ask you to explore a fairly broad area across the three texts. For example:

> **By exploring the writers' methods, compare ideas about the emotional intensity generated by love in one prose text and one poetry text (at least two poems) you have studied.**

There may be a range of poems you could discuss, but you will need to decide quickly which best fit the topic, and which you feel you can explore in sufficient depth. For the purposes of this sample, let us imagine the poems selected are:

Poem A: 'La Belle Dame Sans Merci', John Keats

Poem B: 'The Love Poem', Carol Ann Duffy

Quickly decide which characters and/or relationships you are going to write about in relation to *Wuthering Heights*.

Possible choices:

- Catherine and Heathcliff
- Catherine and Edgar
- Heathcliff and Isabella (if time)

Then decide, or note down, if you have time, some possible ideas related to the three texts:

Wuthering Heights	'La Belle Dame Sans Merci'	'The Love Poem'
• Intensity of the relationship between Catherine and Heathcliff as children • Intensity of the relationship when Catherine meets Heathcliff just before she dies • Catherine's relationship with Edgar • Peace and torment • Heathcliff's treatment of Isabella	• The strangeness of the language of love • The power of dreams and whether this love is real or demonic • The use of nature imagery to describe the effects of love • The impact of the love upon the knight	• The struggle to find a language fit to express this love • The elemental nature of the passion felt • The ending of the poem which takes the lovers beyond this world • Love beyond boundaries and beyond territories

EXAMINER'S TIP

If you are not going to make regular comparisons/ links between the texts, at the very least begin your discussion of **Poem A** with a reference back to *Wuthering Heights*.

Writing your response

Introduction to your response

- Discuss quickly what 'emotional intensity' means, and how well this applies to *Wuthering Heights* and two poems you have studied.

Main body of your response

As you have to write about three texts, in essence, it may not be practical to move between all three in each paragraph or point you make.

- **Start with *Wuthering Heights*** by writing about: **one or more emotionally intense characters or relationships** in the novel and how these are **represented**, for example the relationship between Catherine and Heathcliff which is represented as a wild, free fusion of souls. Key ideas to explore might be:
    - Selfhood as being something other than individualism, but which achieves its true expression in a relationship
    - Death being less of a torment than a life spent separated from one's true love
    - Love extending beyond the grave to haunt the living
    - How these ideas might be seen through the context of the time (for example the conventions of religion and spiritual sensibility that informed much of the Victorian understanding about an afterlife, and particular prisms or critical lenses through which you might read what 'emotional intensity' refers to (i.e. **Romanticism**, ideas about social status, **psychoanalytic readings**, etc.).

- **Write about Poem A**: How is an intense character/relationship or experience represented **similarly or differently** in Poem A? What language, form and structures are used? How does the context in which the poem is read or has been produced affect the interpretation (e.g. does it give the female voice more prominence? Does it deal more directly with the effects of 'intensity'? Why was this done in this way? How does it reflect the writer's interests? What do the critics say? Are there contextual/cultural factors to consider?).

- **Write about Poem B**: Begin by exploring the intense relationship/character or experience in the poem, and then draw **links** or points of **contrast** with both **Poem A** and *Wuthering Heights*. Where you can, draw links across all three – whether that is in voice/perspective or the nature of experience, the tone, mood or approach.

- Write more freely **about any** of the **three texts**: Once you have established the basics: how each text has approached the subject matter, and any clear links or contrasts, then move onto exploring any specific aspects of the three texts you have not addressed so far. If you can, reference at least one of the other texts, e.g. *In the same manner that Heathcliff's all-consuming passion for Catherine is both destructive and inspiring, the speaker of 'La Belle Dame Sans Merci' is drawn to his lover.*

Conclusion

- Synthesise elements of what you have said into a final paragraph that fluently, succinctly and inventively leaves the reader/examiner with the sense that you have engaged with this task and the three texts.

> In 'The Love Poem' Carol Ann Duffy interleaves fragments of other love poems with her own words, suggesting that the expression of true love is the same across all eras, genders and classes. The poem also acknowledges the struggle to find an adequate language in which to express love, which echoes Catherine and Heathcliff's struggle to articulate their love. However, in Keats's 'La Belle Dame sans Merci', the knight's desire leaves him as 'palely loitering' as any of the ghosts in 'Wuthering Heights'.

EXAMINER'S TIP

You could begin with a powerful quotation that you use to launch into your response. For example: *'That is how I'm loved! Well, never mind! That is not my Heathcliff. I shall love mine yet; and take him with me; he's in my soul.'* Catherine's declaration of love for Heathcliff is one that goes beyond human expression to a place of deep corresponding identity, a place that supercedes the boundaries of life and death and can only be understood through the ineffable expression of the soul.

USING CRITICAL INTERPRETATIONS AND PERSPECTIVES

What is a critical interpretation?

The particular way a text is viewed or understood can be called an interpretation, and can be made by literary critics (specialists in studying literary texts), reviewers, or everyday readers and students. It is about taking a position on particular elements of the text, or on what others say about it. For example, you could consider:

1. Notions of 'character'

What **sort/type** of person Heathcliff – or another character – is:

- Is the character an '**archetype**' (a specific type of character with common features)? Heathcliff is often described as the archetypal **Romantic** hero. Professor John Bowen has suggested that Heathcliff embodies the novel's deepest contradictions: he is insider and outsider, remarkably self-controlled and utterly wild. He is both hero and anti-hero.
- Does the character personify, **symbolise** or represent a specific idea or trope (e.g. the **Byronic hero**, the ruthless avenger)?
- Is the character modern, universal, of his/her time, historically accurate, etc.? (For example, might we recognise Heathcliff in some of today's iconic figures?)

2. Ideas and issues

What the novel tells us about **particular ideas or issues** and how we interpret these. For example:

- How society is structured: the complex social hierarchy that exists even between neighbouring farms is integral to Brontë's novel, which explores the subtle negotiations of class, ownership, social status and kinship.
- The role of men/women: Brontë examines and defies common expectations of the qualities proper to masculinity and femininity, both in terms of behaviour and in terms of power.
- Moral codes and social justice: the passionate intensities of the world of *Wuthering Heights* create a space where revenge is uninhibited by ideas of law or justice. Heathcliff's ruthless determination to avenge himself exposes the inadequacies and flaws in the laws of inheritance.

3. Links and contexts

To what extent the novel **links with, follows or pre-echoes** other ideas. For example:

- Catherine's conviction that love can extend beyond boundaries, and even dismantle the boundaries of the self, might be compared to the ways in which Virginia Woolf experiments with time, memory, love and identity in *Mrs Dalloway* (1925).
- Brontë's attention to the place of women in society, which she explores through the issues of marriage and servitude, might be compared with the way in which Khaled Hosseini depicts the role of women in Afghani society in *A Thousand Splendid Suns* (2007).
- Brontë's handling of complex time schemes and shifting **narrative** voices can be compared with Woolf's experimentation with form in *Mrs Dalloway*. Similarly, Woolf explores the boundaries of gender and identity in her novels in ways that were just as astonishing to her contemporary readers as Brontë's bold blurring of traditional gender characteristics in *Wuthering Heights* was to her contemporary readers.

4. Genre and narrative structure

How the novel is **constructed** and how Brontë **makes** her narrative:

- Does it follow particular narrative conventions, or create them? For example, those of the **Gothic genre**?
- What are the functions of specific events, characters, plot devices, locations, etc. in relation to narrative or genre?
- What are the specific moments of tension, conflict, crisis and denouement?

5. Reader responses

How the novel **works on the reader**, and across time and in different contexts:

- How does Brontë **position** the reader? Are we to empathise with, feel distance from, judge and/or evaluate the events and characters?

6. Critical reaction

And, finally, how do different readers view the novel? For example, modernist or postmodern readers in more recent years.

Writing about critical perspectives

The important thing to remember is that **you** are a critic too. Your job is to evaluate what a critic or school of criticism has said about the elements above, arrive at your own conclusions, and also express your own ideas.

In essence, you need to: **consider** the views of others, **synthesise** them, then decide on **your perspective**. For example:

Explain the viewpoints

Critical view A about power:

Feminist readings have contrasted the characterisation of Heathcliff and Edgar Linton in terms of power. Sandra Gilbert offers an intriguing reading of Heathcliff as 'feminine' because he lacks social power.

Critical view B about the same aspect:

Terry Eagleton's Marxist analysis of power in 'Wuthering Heights' focuses on the choice Catherine makes between Heathcliff and Edgar Linton. Eagleton sees this choice in terms of ideology; her choice, which arguably proves fatal, is not prompted by love, Eagleton argues, but by a practical understanding of social power relations.

Then synthesise and add your perspective:

Sandra Gilbert's feminist argument that Heathcliff has no 'masculine power' can be contrasted with Terry Eagleton's comment that 'Catherine rejects Heathcliff as a suitor because he is socially inferior to Linton.' Eagleton sees Heathcliff's lack of power as socially produced. However, one could argue that Heathcliff occupies the most powerful position in the novel, being essential to the development of all the major themes: love, revenge, morality. The power of his love can summon Catherine from the grave. His power over Isabella, Hindley, Linton and Nelly enables him to implement his revenge. Without Heathcliff this novel would be distinctly lacking in power and thematic purpose.

A05 KEY INTERPRETATION

Here are just two examples of different kinds of response to *Wuthering Heights*

Critic 1 – C. P. Sanger's reading of the novel's structure (1926) seeks to distance the novel from some of the moral criticism it had incurred during its early reviews. Rather than looking at whether it was an 'improving' experience to read the novel, Sanger argues that the symmetry of the family relationships and the tightly wrought structure of the novel redeem it from its initial reception as a 'fiend of a book, a monster'. Sanger's critique can be seen as paving the way for critics such as Robert Scholes (*Structuralism in Literature: An Introduction*, 1974) who investigates the complex narrative structure.

Critic 2 – More contemporary critics such as Hillis Miller (1982) also focus on the structure of *Wuthering Heights* but see the repetitions and ruptures in the framing as preventing a single understanding of the novel.

ANNOTATED SAMPLE ANSWERS

Below are extracts from three sample answers at different levels to the same task/question. Bear in mind that these responses may not correspond exactly to the style of question you might face – for example, AO5 is not assessed by Edexcel – but they will give a broad indication of some of the key skills required.

> **By exploring the writers' methods, compare ideas about conflict in relationships in one prose text and one poetry text (at least two poems) you have studied.**

Candidate 1

AO3 Clear opening paragraph making specific reference to the text and also referring to context

It might seem strange that in a love story there would be so many ideas about conflict, but in 'Wuthering Heights' almost all the characters come into conflict with the ideas of the time, or with each other. For example, Catherine is much more free to roam the moors than Victorian women would normally be, and she is very wilful, even violent at times. Examples of this violence, such as when she asks for a whip, have led some feminist critics to say Catherine is quite masculine.

AO5 Awareness of critical views

AO1 Personal viewpoint but informally expressed

While I don't really agree with that view, I do think Catherine is unusually aggressive for a woman of her time, especially when she slaps and is physically violent to the other characters when she does not get her own way. She is a very fiery character, which contrasts with the characters in Elizabeth Jennings's poem 'One Flesh' which is a very cold poem, though the couple are also in conflict.

AO4 Begins to make a useful point of comparison but fails to develop it

AO2 Simple analysis needs further exploration

Interestingly the poem is entitled 'One Flesh' and that is exactly how Catherine describes her relationship with Heathcliff, though there is not much passion left between the two characters in Jennings's poem. Also contrasting with 'Wuthering Heights', the characters in Jennings's poem stay indoors, in bed, which is the direct opposite of Catherine until she is ill, which she becomes because of the conflict she feels in marrying Edgar and loving Heathcliff.

AO2 Insightful point rather clumsily made

AO3 Awareness of social context

The central conflict in the novel is Catherine's choice of who to marry. This was an important choice for Victorian women, because they were dependent on men for their survival. In Victorian times there was a great deal of inequality between men and women, and women didn't have a lot of power. Brontë sets up the choice between Edgar and Heathcliff as though there wasn't really a choice: knowing that financial security is of utmost importance Catherine tells Nelly 'It would degrade me to marry Heathcliff.' But then the plot unfolds to show that really the choice was the other way. It degrades Catherine to marry someone who is not her soul mate. In the end, she is so degraded that she dies and becomes a ghost.

AO1 Good observation with evidence of personal interpretation

AO2 Moves towards answering the question about method here but no discussion of Brontë's techniques

Another love triangle which forms an area of conflict in the novel is when Isabella falls in love with the transformed Heathcliff. Catherine warns Isabella not to love Heathcliff, who she says is a 'fierce, pitiless, wolfish man', but Isabella suspects that this is because Catherine really loves him herself. However, Catherine knows Heathcliff's true nature, which, dominated by his animal quality, is to destroy Isabella. As readers we believe Catherine, but we also know that Isabella has a valid point.

AO4
Useful comparison between texts

The love triangle is also a part of Anne Sexton's poem 'For My Lover, Returning to His Wife' but in this poem the conflict is all internal. The poet gives her lover the permission to return to his wife, even though she wishes she could be more permanent herself. However, in 'Wuthering Heights', Heathcliff cannot give Catherine permission to stay with Edgar – he sees her marriage to Edgar as an act of violence towards himself. And Catherine blames both of them for ruining her. Again we see Catherine as quite a spoiled character, who blames her misfortunes on other people. It is because of this that Nelly Dean, the servant, has no patience with her and fails to see that she is really ill. Catherine's poor behaviour misleads Nelly into thinking she is pretending and so contributes to her own death.

AO1
Attempt at analysis but not clearly linked to question

AO3
Awareness of literary movements, rather simplistic understanding

Another area of conflict in this novel is the conflict between religion and love. Brontë presents a version of traditional Christianity which is almost laughable in the character of Joseph. Joseph is rude and grudging. He is not nice to any of the other characters, and almost delights in their misfortunes. Against this, Brontë puts forward the idea of a more Romantic kind of love, the love between Catherine and Heathcliff, which she says is itself a kind of truth, and morally good. This can be seen also in Blake's poetry. Blake did not like the dominant Christian views expressed by the Church during his lifetime. His poem 'The Garden of Love' mentions a garden full of graves, all thorny and covered in briars. Like Brontë he concludes that if true love is unacceptable in Victorian society, it is capable of killing you. However, Brontë goes beyond this because she says that true love extends even beyond the grave.

AO1
Simplistic analysis which verges on misunderstanding the metaphorical value of the poem

AO1
Rather brief conclusion though it does refer back to the question

In conclusion, Brontë and a number of poets have all chosen to write about love through a series of conflicts; for them the business of love is a heart-searching and potentially life-threatening affair, capable of leaving you out in the cold, and rejected by society.

MID LEVEL

Comment

- AO1 A clear and methodical approach, weighing up evidence in a basic but consistent way. Needs to push the analysis further to move it beyond broad observations, but the fundamentals of critical reading are in place. Points are not always relevant to the question or developed thoroughly, and expression is rather informal at times.

- AO2 The writer exhibits some sense of the ways in which meaning is shaped in *Wuthering Heights* and the poems. A more sustained attention to language and technique, and improved expression would have raised the level of the analysis.

- AO3 Makes reference to historical context but critical engagement with it needs further development. Not absolutely relevant to the question as it stands so the argument needs to be made more thoroughly.

- AO4 Connections with other literary texts are made but are rather simplistic – could be further developed.

- AO5 This answer demonstrates a basic critical understanding of the texts and an ability to read them sensitively. It fails to engage with more sophisticated critical perspectives.

To improve the answer:

- Pay closer attention to the way meaning may be shaped by use of language and literary techniques. (AO2)

- Engage more purposefully with relevant historical and literary contexts. (AO3/AO4)

- Develop a more sophisticated understanding of how critical interpretations might shed light on key issues. (AO5)

Candidate 2

Although 'Wuthering Heights' has been called the world's greatest love story, it is nevertheless a novel fraught with clashing relationships. Indeed, with the possible exception of Nelly's relationships with all the characters, there isn't one that isn't shot through with conflict. Conflict is at the heart of this novel, and Brontë appears to view it in different ways. For instance, the conflict between Heathcliff and Catherine represents the passion of their relationship yet the conflict between Isabella and Heathcliff merely indicates how totally ill-suited they are to each other. Much of the conflict in the novel can be put down to class divisions. Heathcliff comes into the family house from the outside, having been found on the streets in Liverpool: he belongs nowhere, is possibly illegitimate, has no property, not even his own name. Mr Earnshaw's preference for this 'poor fatherless child' sows the seeds of conflict which will grow throughout the novel. Right from the beginning then we can see that there is a potential conflict with the arrival of an unwanted child.

This struggle reflects the social conditions of the time. The novel was written during the Industrial Revolution, a time of great social upheaval, when out of conflict came greatness, and new technologies. There were also lots of children left abandoned or orphaned on the streets because of enormous inner city poverty. A novel clearly enables the writer to develop conflict over time, laying its foundations and then building on them as the novel progresses. In poetry, establishing conflict has to be done much more economically, but it is interesting that the Metaphysical poet Andrew Marvell in his poem 'To His Coy Mistress' uses the concept of time to establish the idea of conflict 'Had we but World enough, and Time, This coyness Lady were no crime.' Marvell is at the mercy of time, not only as a lover, but also as a poet. The conflict he feels makes the need to express his love more urgent. The poem goes on to detail how much the poet desires his mistress, but because of social conventions about what is acceptable behaviour, and because time is not on their side, he feels in danger of losing her, as he says in despair: 'And your quaint Honour turn to dust; and into ashes all my Lust.' This last quotation also suggests that his love has boundaries, and cannot extend beyond death, which contrasts with the passion between Catherine and Heathcliff.

Anne Sexton's poem 'For My Lover, Returning to His Wife' uses a series of metaphors and similes for establishing the conflict in the poet's heart when she considers the wife, whom she describes as being like fireworks or a cooking pot. There is something brilliant about the wife, with which she cannot compete, and she is also undeniably real, solid and practical. Brontë also makes use of metaphor and simile for describing the conflicting passions which Catherine feels for her lover (Heathcliff) and her husband (Edgar) 'The contrast resembled what you see in exchanging a bleak, hilly, coal country for a beautiful fertile valley.' The use of nature imagery here suggests the different qualities of the two men: Heathcliff is bleak but solid, with hidden depths that may yet bring riches; Edgar is softer, aesthetically pleasing, and fertile. These suggestively contrasting descriptions developed as the novel progresses.

A01 Good use of embedded quotation to explore the question, and a sign of critical thinking

A02 Clear opening paragraph, making specific reference to the text, and suggesting an understanding of how meaning is created by the author

A03 Demonstrates an understanding of the social conditions during which the novel was produced

A04 Creative link between the two texts

A04 Good exploration of connections between literary texts, which could have been explored further

A01 Good use of quotation, basic critical understanding employing accurate knowledge of literary terms

In 'Wuthering Heights', Brontë is able to develop a much more complex and contrasting account of the various conflicts between the characters. For instance, when Catherine is courting Edgar in Volume I, there is a clear conflict of wills between herself and Edgar. Edgar's basic powerlessness is remarked upon by Nelly 'he's doomed, and flies to his fate', but what sets the tone of the whole passage is the underlying violence that simmers throughout.

Anne Sexton hints at violence in only one stanza in her poem, but the sentiment is just as dark, and we are in no doubt as to the power of the poet's feelings. The reference to the wife as a cooking pot puts her firmly in the kitchen, as the traditional idea of a woman's place, but the word 'fireworks' makes it seem like the poet herself would like to occupy that place.

A01

Basic but clear evidence of critical thinking

So, the conflict comes from a clash of personalities in Brontë's case, but it is also a conflict that arises because of power and social class. Catherine chooses to marry Edgar because without him she is reduced to poverty. This highlights an issue that is also relevant in Sexton's poem: the power of women. Catherine's conflict comes because she does not have the power to make her own choice. Society has decided that in order for her to survive she has to marry someone who has property. Similarly in Sexton's poem, the mistress has no power, no substance of her own – she washes off like watercolour paint.

A05

A good concluding paragraph that makes an attempt to outline the different methods used by the different writers, and has a basis in a critical understanding of those methods

To conclude, the three different writers explore conflict in different ways across the centuries. In the seventeenth century, Andrew Marvell uses a courtly language full of extravagant images to persuade his reluctant mistress to compensate for the conflict he feels and let their passion be physical. In the nineteenth century, Brontë focuses on issues of class, social status and sexual passion in order to establish the complex layers of conflict which motivate her characters. And in the twentieth century, Anne Sexton uses the confessional mode to expose the internal conflict that the poet feels in an unequal relationship with her lover and his wife.

GOOD LEVEL

Comment

- AO1 A creative and carefully thought out answer with good evidence of a personal understanding of the texts in question.
- AO2 An engagement with the mechanics of literary method enables an examination of the different ways in which meanings are produced.
- AO3 Good choice of poems to compare different ways in which context influences the production of ideas.
- AO4 Good links between the texts, drawing out new insights.
- AO5 An acknowledgement that different critical perspectives are invited by this text, with leanings toward (rather than real engagement with) narrative theory.

To improve the answer:

- A more thorough investigation as to the methods writers use to produce meaning would have answered the demands of the question more fully. (AO2)
- Elaborate and expand the references to historical and literary contexts. (AO3/AO4)
- Sharpen the sense of how a critical perspective shapes the interpretation of a text. (AO5)

Candidate 3

A01

Confidently personal and creative first paragraph establishing how this question might be engaged with

'Wuthering Heights' portrays a society that is in profound conflict with its ideas about how people can and should relate to each other. Central to an understanding of the text is our response to the question about what is proper and what is not. Where we stand on this simply articulated conflict determines how we will respond to the disturbances of the uncanny, how we will respond to the violations of the family, and how we will react to the choices that Catherine makes and the consequences of those choices for herself and the other characters in the novel.

From the beginning of the novel, Catherine, who is described as 'headstrong and domineering' by Nelly, challenges all our certainties about boundaries and convention. She appears to us first as a palimpsest, a series of self-contradictory written names in the flyleaf of a book. She appears not in person, but in name: the power of the word evokes her. And when we do encounter her, Brontë presents her as a frightening little child ghost: 'a changeling', a 'wicked little soul' who haunts the property of Wuthering Heights, longing to be loved, longing to be 'let in' almost as though she is asking to be let into the interior narrative of the novel. Right from the start, Brontë encourages us to see Catherine, the central figure of love interest in the novel, as disruptive, disturbing and possibly violent.

A01

Good analysis, correct use of literary terminology

A04

Well expressed summary of ideas

A05

Confident use of quotation to support a complex point. Good use of critical material

The critic C. P. Sanger has written extensively on the structure of 'Wuthering Heights' and suggests that it is a book of 'remarkable symmetries' and precise topographies. It is noteworthy then, in a novel where the author has taken such care to get the structure and setting so absolute, and so strictly accurate, that there are so many discrepancies or conflicts which disturb our readings of this love story and the relationships within it.

Catherine is 'wilful' and 'wild' and she has a 'fierce temper' yet she nevertheless feels compelled to marry not for love but for propriety. The novel may have at its heart a love story, but it is one fraught with violence and Gothic terror. And those who are educated (Lockwood, Edgar) are no better at reading the world of the novel than those who are 'wild' or 'unreclaimed' (Catherine, Heathcliff).

A04

Effective change of focus to introduce new ideas

One of the central conflicts between the characters in this novel is between those who belong and those who do not. This is exemplified in the contrasting accounts of the two narrators: Lockwood, the outsider, and Nelly Dean, the garrulous but shrewd interior narrator. Lockwood's accounts are superceded by Nelly's and so his assumptions about character and landscape, are therefore overwritten and refined by her corrective versions. His assumed intellectual and social superiority is exposed through this method as being baseless and self-serving. It is tempting to scoff at Lockwood's inability to read the social language of the novel, but Brontë suggests that we are just as prone to misreading as he is, and that even Catherine will fall to the temptations of understanding the world in conventional rather than authentically truthful ways.

A02

Powerfully expressed argument which combines a personal reading with an understanding of how authors shape meaning

Catherine chooses to marry Edgar over Heathcliff, because 'he is handsome, and young, and cheerful, and rich' but she declares only a few paragraphs later 'In my

A05

Good critical point, forcefully made

soul and in my heart, I'm convinced I'm wrong!' Both Marxist and feminist readings of this choice have focused on the social limitations under which Catherine is operating as she makes her decision. But Catherine is clear, she knows that there is a moral conflict at the heart of her choosing. And because this is a moral conflict, Catherine is also clear about its consequences: when she makes it she will not be fit for heaven.

Something similar inflects the relationship between the lover and her beloved in Carol Ann Duffy's poem 'The Love Poem'. This is a poem which is written around the impossibility of expressing love: love can be known by heart, learned like a prayer but ultimately whether it is something best expressed in the mind or by the pen, it becomes lost in half written, half remembered lines.

Like Brontë, Duffy uses the literary device of the palimpsest to layer up and disturb singular meanings. She quotes other lines, articulates into her poem great love poems from other eras, to try and express love, but love she avers is annihilating of language, and ultimately annihilating of the self. The desire Duffy describes in the poem is not just the commonplace desire of the moth for the flame, but for something otherworldly, beyond time and space, something that burns far more brightly than a flame. Both writers suggest that love goes beyond the normal realm, and extends beyond what can properly be articulated in language.

A04

Excellent point of comparison

This expression of a love which is beyond the normal realm of experience, which is not subject to the constraints of the ordinary, extends right back to Shakespeare's Sonnet 116 which begins 'Let me not to the marriage of true minds. Admit impediments.' In Brontë's novel, however, the marriage of true minds, in other words, Catherine's and Heathcliff's, would have been beset by impediments, not least the reduction of their social status to destitution. Like Shakespeare, Brontë posits a love that defies time, a love that is borne even 'to the edge of doom', a love that is understood in terms of the sublime, but for Brontë this love is in conflict with the social mores of the rather narrow rural Victorian community of the novel.

A03

Impressive comparison, acknowledging cultural context

A05

Excellent comparison points and awareness of critical standpoint

A feminist critic might point out that for Shakespeare, love comes unconflicted by social mores and unmoved by either natural phenomena or the laws of physics. Both Brontë and Duffy recognise aspects of this love in their writing, but both of them express the suffering that comes from recognising such a love but being unable to fulfil it within the constraints of their different social and literary environments. In different ways they express those conflicts in terms of the supernatural, or ghostly echoes from other eras. For Brontë, love is transgressive, intense and demonic; for Duffy, it is annihilatory, overlaid by other expressions, other approximations and declarations of desire, but truly and finally, only to be experienced as an incendiary consummation of the self.

A04

Creative and persuasive response to the question thoroughly exploring the connections between the different literary texts.

VERY HIGH LEVEL

Comment

- AO1 An impressively argued and creatively personal and insightful response.
- AO2 Confident use of quotations reflecting a fundamental understanding of how meaning is created in the text.
- AO3 Good choice of secondary literary texts suggesting an understanding of how historical context influences writing.
- AO4 Confident use of literary material to explore the student's own critical response to the texts.
- AO5 Judicious reference to critical approaches and the light they might shed on central issues of the text.

PRACTICE TASK

Now it's your turn to work through an exam-style task on *Wuthering Heights*. The key is to:

- Quickly read and decode the task/question
- Briefly plan your points – then add a few more details, such as evidence, or make links between them
- Write your answer

Decode the question

Compare the ways in which the writers of your two chosen texts present women's struggle for identity. You must relate your discussion to relevant contextual factors.

'women's struggle for identity'	Define the terms: what is identity? Description of limitations of patriarchy; descriptions of the ways in which the women struggle. To what extent are they successful?
'relevant contextual factors'	Historical context? Cultural context? Political or **ideological** context?

Plan and write

- Decide your viewpoint
- Plan your points
- Think of key evidence and quotations
- Write your answer

Success criteria

- Show your understanding of the idea of individual identity
- Draw on a range of critical views or different interpretations as appropriate
- Sustain your focus on the idea of 'struggle for identity'
- Argue your point of view clearly and logically
- Make perceptive points and express your ideas confidently
- Support your points with relevant, well-chosen evidence including quotations
- Use literary terminology accurately and appropriately with reference to the effect on the reader
- Write in fluent, controlled and accurate English

Once you have finished, use the **Mark scheme** on page 128 to evaluate your response.

EXAMINER'S TIP

Remember to incorporate the views of critics and other writers, but make sure that the central idea is your own. For example, *A psychoanalytical reading of Brontë's novel focuses on her use of dreams. Such readings argue that dreams reveal both the personal unconscious and the 'unconscious' of the novel. Thus, Lockwood's two dreams reveal the novel's central mystery: when Catherine's ghost taps at the window, something inadmissible is erupting: that which is repressed will rise to the surface and must be faced before the social issues of the novel can be resolved.*

FURTHER READING

Works

Emily Brontë, *The Complete Poems*, ed. Derek Roper with Edward Chitham, Clarendon Press, 1995

Biography

Juliet Barker, *The Brontës,* Weidenfield & Nicolson, 1994, reprinted 2010

Katherine Frank, *Emily Brontë: A Chainless Soul*, H. Hamilton, 1990; paperback, Penguin Books, Harmondsworth, 1992

Elizabeth Gaskell, *The Life of Charlotte Brontë*, Smith, Elder & Co., London, 1857; reprinted by Penguin Books, 1975

Winifred Gérin, *Emily Brontë*, Clarendon Press, 1971

A. Mary F. Robinson, *Emily Brontë*, W. H. Allen, 1883

Critical works

Miriam Allott, ed., *The Brontës: The Critical Heritage*, Routledge & Kegan Paul, 1974

Nancy Armstrong, 'Imperialist Nostalgia and *Wuthering Heights'*, in Linda H. Peterson, ed., *Wuthering Heights: Case Studies in Contemporary Criticism*, 1992

Trevor J. Barnes and James S. Duncan, eds, *Writing Worlds: Discourse, Text and Metaphor in the Respresentation of Landscape*, Routledge & Kegan Paul, 1992

Harold Bloom, ed., *Emily Brontë's Wuthering Heights,* Chelsea, 1987

Ian Brinton, *Brontë's Wuthering Heights: Reader's Guides*, Continuum International Publishing Group, 2010

Lord David Cecil, *Early Victorian Novelists: Essays in Revaluation*, revised edition, University of Chicago Press, 1958; originally published 1935

Susan Chaplin,*York Notes Companions: Gothic Literature,* York Press & Longman, 2011

Jay Clayton, *Romantic Vision and The Novel*, Cambridge University Press, 1987

Claire Colebrook, *New Literary Histories: New Historicism and Contemporary Criticism*, Manchester University Press, 1997

Sydney Dobell, 'Currer Bell and *Wuthering Heights'*, *Palladium* (September 1850)

Clare B. Dunkle, 'The Mysteries of Wuthering Heights', www.claredunkle.com/Design/maidsbrmysteries.htm, New York 2010

Terry Eagleton, *Myths of Power: A Marxist Study of the Brontës*, Harper & Row, 1975, 2nd edition, Macmillan, 1992

Eva Figes, *Sex and Subterfuge, Women Writers in 1850*, Pandora, 1982

Juliann E. Fleenor, ed., *The Female Gothic*, Eden Press, 1983

Sigmund Freud, *The Interpretation of Dreams*, Penguin; first Penguin edition 1953

Barbara Gates, 'Victorian Suicide: Mad Crimes and Sad Histories', www.victorianweb.org/books/suicide/02.html

Sandra Gilbert and Susan Gubar, *The Madwoman in the Attic: The Woman Writer and the Nineteenth-Century Literary Imagination*, Yale University Press, 1979

Margaret Homans, 'Dreaming of Children: Literalization in *Jane Eyre* and *Wuthering Heights'*, in Juliann E. Fleenor, ed., *The Female Gothic*, Eden Press, 1983 (see above)

E. Jolly, ed., *The Life and Letters of Sydney Dobell*, volume 1, Smith, 1878

Frank Kermode, *The Classic*, Faber & Faber, 1975

Robert Kiely, *The Romantic Novel in England*, Harvard University Press, 1972

Sheryl Mann, 'In Defense of Isabella Linton: An Analysis of her Role in *Wuthering Heights* as a Foil to Catherine Earnshaw', uscupstate.edu/mannsj/wutheringheights.html 2012

Nicholas Marsh, *Emily Brontë: Wuthering Heights*, Analysing Texts, Macmillan, 1999

J. Hillis Miller, *Fiction and Repetition*, Harvard University Press and Basil Blackwell, 1982

Sara Mills, Lynne Pearce, Susan Spaull, Elaine Millard, eds, *Feminist Readings, Feminists Reading*, Harvester Wheatsheaf, 1989

Linda H. Peterson, ed., *Wuthering Heights: Case Studies in Contemporary Criticism*, Bedford Books of St Martin's Press, 1992

Ruth Robbins, *Literary Feminisms*, Macmillan, 2000

Rick Rylance, ed., *Debating Texts*, OUP, 1987

C. P. Sanger, 'The Structure of "Wuthering Heights"', *Hogarth Essays XIX*, Hogarth Press, 1926

Mark Schorer, 'Fiction and the Matrix of Analogy', *Kenyon Review* 11:4 (Autumn 1949)

Allan Lloyd Smith, *Modern Gothic: A Reader*, Manchester University Press, 1996

Clifton Snider, '"The Imp of Satan"; The Vampire Archetype in *Wuthering Heights* and *Jane Eyre*', https://webcsulb.edu/~csnider/brontes.html, August 2009

Susan Sontag, *Illness as Metaphor and AIDS and its Metaphors*, Penguin, 1991

Patsy Stoneman, ed., *Wuthering Heights: Contemporary Critical Essays*, Macmillan, 1993

Julia Swindells, *Victorian Writing and Working Women*, University of Minnesota Press, 1985

Dorothy Van Ghent, *The English Novel: Form and Function*, Harper Torchbooks, 1961

Marina Warner, *From the Beast to the Blonde*, Chatto & Windus, 1994

Raymond Williams, *The Country and the City*, Chatto & Windus, 1973

Philip K. Wion, 'The Absent Mother in Emily Brontë's *Wuthering Heights*', *American Imago* 42 (1985)

Julian Wolfreys, *Transgression: Identity, Space, Time,* Palgrave Macmillan Transitions Series, 2008

LITERARY TERMS

anecdote secret or unpublished **narratives**; the narrative of a striking event

archetype a standard character type showing typical traits, e.g. the vampire, the hero

biographical theory a critical approach which focuses upon the relationship between fiction and reality by drawing upon the author's life story

Byronic hero characteristically both glamorous and dangerous, haunted by the guilt of mysterious crimes

deconstruction a **post-structuralist** approach to literature initiated by the theoretical ideas of Jacques Derrida. Deconstruction posits the radical undecidability of all texts

destabilising to make uncertain, to unsettle meaning

dialect a regional variety of English distinguished by pronunciation, vocabulary or grammar

discourse discourse theory is associated with the writings of Michel Foucault. Discourse generally refers to the language in which a specific area of knowledge is discussed, e.g. the discourse of law or medicine

eponymous relating to or being the person or thing after which something is named

feminist criticism there are many different forms of feminist criticism: some critics suggest ways of reading which draw attention to the patriarchal assumptions underpinning cultural production; others focus on the rediscovery of works by women writers; still others concentrate on the psychological and linguistic opportunities for women in a male-dominated culture

formalism also known as **new criticism**; formalists concentrate on the formal structure of the text, particularly such elements as imagery, symbolism, repetition

frame narrative a story that encloses another story

genre a style, category or classification of literature (or any of the arts)

Gothic a genre of writing which has a number of typical elements such ghosts, horror, **sublime** landscapes

gynocriticism a term which refers to the practice of turning away from the analysis of male-authored texts to an analysis of female-authored texts and their specific differences from one another

hegemony associated with the political writings of Antonio Gramsci, hegemony refers to the web of **ideologies** that shape people's view of the world

ideology a set of beliefs about the world which seems both natural and inevitable

Marxist criticism a way of reading texts that focuses upon their material and historical conditions

metaphor a figure of speech in which a word or phrase is applied to an object, a character or an action which does not literally belong to it, in order to imply a resemblance and create an unusual or striking image in the reader's mind

metaphysical visionary writing, generally associated with the seventeenth century; incorporeal, abstract

narrative a story, tale or any recital of events, and the manner in which it is told. First person narratives ('I') are told from the character's perspective and usually require the reader to judge carefully what is being said; second person narratives ('you') suggest the reader is part of the story; in third person narratives ('he', 'she', 'they'), the **narrator** may be intrusive (continually commenting on the story), impersonal or omniscient (all knowing). More than one style or narrative may be used in a text

narrator the voice telling the story or relating a sequence of events

new criticism see **formalism**

new historicism a form of criticism heavily influenced by **Marxist criticism** and the work of Michel Foucault. Foucault's notions of 'power' and 'discourse' were particularly formative of new historicist thinking

novel of manners late eighteenth-century literary genre which deals with the conflict between individual aspirations and the accepted codes of social behaviour. There is a vital relationship between social behaviour, manners and character. Manners have a moral value, as well as a social value in this genre

palimpsest a text that is overwritten with other **narratives** and messages

parable a story which explains something that cannot easily be described otherwise

paradox a statement that contradicts itself and yet seems true

pathetic fallacy the attribution of human feelings to objects in nature and, commonly, weather systems, so that the mood of the **narrator** or the characters can be discerned from the behaviour of the surrounding environment

plurality a large number of things, or ways of viewing a text

post-structuralism both a continuation and a critique of **structuralism**. Post-structuralist criticism expands the possibilities of language: the binary oppositions central to a **structuralist** position proliferate into innumerable alternatives. In post-structuralist readings meaning is never stable and uncontrovertible, but always provisional and contradictory

pseudonym an adopted name under which to write

psychoanalytic criticism a way of considering texts in terms of the psychoanalytic theories of Sigmund Freud. Emphasis upon dream analysis. Later psychoanalytic theory takes account of the work of Jacques Lacan, especially his theories of language

rhetorical question a question that requires no answer but is formulated as a question to produce a dramatic effect

Romantic a literary form characterised by a conscious preoccupation with the subjective and imaginative aspects of life

structural opposition from the teachings of Ferdinand de Saussure. Saussure's general conclusion is that 'in a language there are only differences, without positive terms'. In other words, meaning comes from difference and does not occur in the terms themselves. The differences are conceived of as structural oppositions, i.e. we understand cold because it is not hot

structuralism structuralist criticism derives from the linguistic theory of Saussure. It focuses on the internal structures of language which permit a text to 'mean' something. A structuralist analysis posits language rather than an individual author as the creator of meaning: no word has intrinsic meaning, in and of itself – it only means something in relation to other words. This insight is discussed chiefly in terms of binary oppositions. We understand what 'hot' means only in relation to the term 'cold'. According to structuralists, writing has no origin – every individual utterance is already preceded by language

sublime quality of awesome grandeur, as distinguished from the beautiful, in nature

symbolic, symbolism investing material objects with abstract powers and meanings greater than their own; allowing a complex idea to be represented by a single object

theme a central subject or topic of the text

transcendent often synonymous with **metaphysical** – that which is beyond the limits of human knowledge; exceeding or surpassing the ordinary

REVISION TASK ANSWERS

Task 1: Repetition

- The same characteristics have different impacts in different generations: compare Catherine and Cathy – steadfastness, wilfulness; Edgar Linton and Linton Heathcliff – weakness, illness; Linton and Heathcliff – masculinity, cruelty.
- Catherine's name is repeated in the book Lockwood finds in the room at Wuthering Heights, with her various surnames.
- Both homes are depicted as prisons: Catherine at Thrushcross Grange; Cathy at Wuthering Heights.
- Animals, and dogs in particular, appear in both volumes: what do they represent? Whips, guns and knives are all used as phallic symbols denoting power: who has the power? Who wants it? Literature and books are used to represent knowledge and refinement, and a different kind of power.

Task 2: Religion

- Dreams enable Brontë to write about religion in ways that were subversive and challenging to conventional ideas.
- Joseph's rough dialect and his stern and uncompromising traditional view of religion present a religious sensibility that is almost incomprehensible.
- Catherine and Heathcliff's religious sensibilities contrast with conventional religion.
- Edgar Linton articulates a refined, conventional view of religion but shows no forgiveness to his sister and is threatened by Catherine's passionate views.
- Nelly Dean represents a practical Christianity, laced with superstition and tempered by common sense.

Task 3: Class and empathy

- Lockwood's relationship with Nelly Dean and the residents of Wuthering Heights shows his pomposity and lack of empathy.
- The character of Catherine and the impact of her experiences at Thrushcross Grange show the contrast between the Heights and the Grange and Catherine's transformation.
- The relationship between Cathy and Hareton suggests empathy and love can triumph over class.
- Heathcliff arrives as a foundling and ends up in control of both houses but demonstrates no empathy for any of the other characters apart from Catherine.

Task 4: Mental health

- Catherine, who is described as robust, only becomes ill with brain fever when, after having seen Heathcliff again, her marriage to Edgar is revealed to her as inauthentic and superficial.
- Hindley's addictions and lack of social stability leave him vulnerable to Heathcliff.
- Catherine's death derails Heathcliff's social ambitions and desires for revenge and leaves him only hopeful of being reunited with her in death.

Task 5: Brontë's representations of nature

- The landscape acts as an indicator of both mood and character. Brontë takes sensual pleasure in the landscape.
- People are described as lambs, wolves, dogs and bears, and take on those animal characteristics. This can serve to dehumanise them, or make them less civilised and less responsible for their behaviours.
- Characters are defined according to whether they belong inside or out. Linton and Cathy's meeting on the moors is an example of how the landscape facilitates their deception. It is easy for Linton to appear more frail than he is, simply because he is outside of his own environment.

Task 6: An unreliable narrator

- There is a discrepancy between Lockwood's narrative and Nelly Dean's: for example, his first analysis of the character of Heathcliff.
- Lockwood's inability to read landscape, both literal and social, suggests a limited viewpoint.
- Lockwood tends to jump to conclusions about both characters and situations: Heathcliff, Cathy, the pile of rabbits. This shows his lack of awareness, sensitivity and judgement.

Task 7: Dreams and the supernatural

- Lockwood's dreams of Catherine and of the Branderham sermon set up the conflicts between belonging and exclusion; religion and truth; violence and forgiveness.
- Catherine's dream of heaven unnerves Nelly (why?) and reveals her subconscious desires. The dream depicts notions of heaven and hell as a moral choice between conventional marriage and authentic love.
- Is the ghost of Catherine tapping at the window 'real' or is it a dream? Who believes in it?
- The final image of the novel is of the little boy who sees the ghosts of Catherine and Heathcliff on the nab. Both Nelly and Lockwood respond to this.

Task 8: Two different worlds

- There are contrasting descriptions of both the houses and the characters: refined/rustic; civilised/wild.
- There are differences in the treatment of women: Catherine and Cathy, and Isabella.
- There are differences in faith and religion at the two locations: Joseph has a puritanical and punitive view of religion; Edgar Linton has a tolerant and hopeful view of faith, but this can be compared with his vindictive and judgmental reaction to Isabella.

PROGRESS CHECK ANSWERS

Part Two: Studying *Wuthering Heights*

Section One: Check your understanding

1.
- Joseph's surly and hard-line religious dogmatism (p. 21) and Lockwood's troubled dream of the Branderham sermon (p. 22–3): in both these instances Brontë gives a view of traditional religion as stern and uncompromising.
- Catherine's anguished dream that 'heaven did not seem to be [her] home' (p. 81): here Brontë suggests that we can make a heaven on earth if only we can be permitted to love each other truly.
- The descriptions of Cathy as a 'little witch' and a 'beneficent fairy' (pp. 14–15) posit an older, more rural religion running against the grain of traditional Christianity.

2.
- The characters are situated in the very particular landscape of the moorlands of the West Riding. From the outset we learn that Lockwood is an 'outsider', not least because he fails to read the signs of the landscape, calling it initially a 'beautiful country' and a 'misanthropist's Heaven' (p. 3) and then commenting on its 'bitter, northern skies, and impassable roads' (p. 91).
- Catherine's love of the landscape which is threaded through the novel establishes her as belonging in a deep and spiritual way to the land.
- The environments with which we associate the Lintons are the parks and gardens, those spaces that have been tamed and civilised.

3.
- It is, of course, both – it is a novel that bristles with the dead, and with ghosts, from Catherine to the unnamed ghosts at the very end of the novel which cause the little shepherd boy to cry.
- Without the ghosts, the novel could not be considered such a passionate love story because Heathcliff's love for Catherine transcends death and transgresses the boundaries of the grave.
- It is also an anti-love story and an anti-ghost story, for the ghosts are all at one remove, being locked into either Lockwood's or Nelly's narratives, and so the chilling pleasures of the traditional horror and suspense of the ghost story are withheld.

4.
- Brontë's use of animal imagery is sustained and complex.
- It is used to suggest an uncivilised character: Heathcliff is described as a 'mad dog' (p. 162).
- Weakness: Lockwood describes himself as 'feeble as a kitten' (p. 32).
- Meekness: as a child Heathcliff is 'as uncomplaining as a lamb' (p. 38) which endears him to Nelly.
- She also uses it to deride social hierarchy: 'Your type is not a lamb, it's a sucking leveret.' (p. 115).
- It is also used to suggest ungovernable passion, as when Isabella is referred to as a vixen (p. 106).

5.
- Physical illness operates to show mental distress or social dislocation. Catherine can never be well at Thrushcross Grange because it is not where she truly belongs.
- Physical sickness also signifies the depth of love that Catherine feels for Heathcliff; her love proves fatal.
- It is also a signifier for femininity or weakness, particularly seen when considering Linton's poor health.
- Catherine's robust good health as a child is in direct opposition to her femininity and womanhood.

6.
- Nelly likes Heathcliff, in spite of herself. Initially because he is uncomplaining and stoical, which are qualities she admires (and can be contrasted with the contempt she feels for Lockwood) but also because he has a charisma to which both she and Isabella respond in different ways.
- Catherine loves him in a different way. Her passion for him is excessive and exhausting to her, but again she cannot resist it.
- He is also described as 'an evil beast' (p. 107) and a 'diabolical man' (p. 222) when he is entirely subject to the trajectory of his own revenge.

7.
- We first encounter her in her letters and notebooks, a confessional account of the early days after her father's death. This segues into her ghost wailing at Lockwood's bedroom window. Both of these descriptions establish a great grief at the heart of Catherine.
- Nelly's description of her at the age of six being able to ride 'any horse in the stable' (p. 36) and choosing a whip as a gift establishes her wild nature, and suggests a tendency to dominance, masculinity and freedom. She is also described as 'mischievous and wayward' (p. 38).
- Her bravery when she is attacked by the Linton's guard dog is contrasted with the 'cowardly' Linton children (p. 50).
- Her behaviour when she returns from Thrushcross Grange is haughty and rude, respresenting the worst of both houses.
- Her tendency to be beset by powerful emotions over which she has little control persists throughout her part in the novel.

8.
- The whole novel is predicated on the idea of family, who belongs and who is excluded.
- The predominance of family names suggests the complex layered nuances of what constitutes family. Heathcliff is given a family name, but not a surname, so he both is and is not of the family.
- The complex laws of inheritance, which are tied up with the position of women in the family, are the mechansim by which Heathcliff is able to exact his revenge.

9.
- Joseph's use of almost impenetrable dialect establishes him as resistant to change, deeply embedded in the ways of his society and reluctant to engage with outsiders or new discourses.
- Lockwood's references to literature and classical architecture situate him as external to the 'natural' environment in which he finds himself. It also establishes him as prejudiced and rude.
- Nelly's ability to speak both languages as an equal, the discourse of the servant and 'mother figure' to Catherine and Heathcliff, coupled with her confident responses to Lockwood and the dominant male characters establishes her as uniquely placed to offer information.

10.

- She believes them to be among the beings who observe the works of mere mortals, as when she tells Hindley 'I wonder his mother does not rise from her grave to see how you use him' when he is cruel to Hareton (p. 76).
- When Catherine is gravely ill and suggests to Nelly that she has seen ghosts and that her room is haunted, Nelly firmly contradicts this, telling her 'It was *yourself*' (p. 123).
- At the end of the novel she tells Lockwood that she believes 'the dead are at peace, but it is not right to speak of them with levity.' (p. 337) which is typical of her subtlety, and her nuanced understanding of the power of things beyond rational explanation.
- When Heathcliff threatens to haunt her after his death, she tells him 'plainly' (p. 334) that his strange talk frightens her.

11.

- Although it has many elements of the Gothic novel: ghosts, repetitions, dreams, isolated buildings and hostile landscapes, it is not Gothic in the precise sense of the term since its ghosts seem to have more to do with romance and passion than with evil.
- Nevertheless the novel has a distinct sense of the uncanny, and a good number of its characters, both educated and roughly born, believe in and are frightened of ghosts.

12.

- It is a parable demonstrating that love is an overarching principle, which is unbounded by merely human events such as death.
- It can also be read as a parable of loss, and lost innocence: the impact of the crushing restrictions of society.
- It might also be considered a parable of survival: what kind of love survives? Who survives?

13.

- Violence in this novel almost always suggests authenticity and true feeling, from Lockwood's real terror as he holds the ghost's wrists over a broken pane of glass through to Heathcliff's violence towards Isabella.
- Catherine's request of the present of a whip as a child is indicative of the inherent violence in her nature. What she is given, instead of the whip, is Heathcliff, and we are already from the beginning encouraged to consider him as potentially violent.
- Many of the instances of violence are sadistically cruel, especially those wrought upon Heathcliff by Hindley and then upon Isabella and Cathy by Heathcliff.

14.

- Catherine's dilemma about who she will choose to marry is stark. She can marry Edgar for security or she can follow her heart and choose Heathcliff, and they will both be penniless.
- She chooses Edgar and persuades herself that this choice is in Heathcliff's interests as well as her own (p. 82), which Nelly tells her is the worst motive yet for marrying Edgar.
- Brontë uses Nelly to outline for Catherine the 'duties' undertaken in marriage, and it is clear that although herself unmarried Nelly has a clear view of the limitations of the options available to a woman such as Catherine.

15.

- Nearly all the action of the novel is prompted by the desire of one character or another for revenge.
- The introduction of Heathcliff into the household was an act of unconditional love or charity by Mr Earnshaw.
- Love is pitted against revenge in a number of ways: Cathy's loving nature, for example, seems to triumph over Heathcliff's determination to wreak his revenge, and even he in the end is defeated in his ambitions by his exhausting love of Catherine.

16.

- Food and starvation are part of the metaphoric life of the novel right from the beginning. Heathcliff is rescued from starvation when he is brought to Wuthering Heights as a foundling.
- The kitchen is one of the main settings of the novel and much of the passionate and violent action takes place there.
- Refusing to eat is also of significance. Catherine refuses to eat for grief and sorrow, and starves; Linton refuses the porridge Joseph serves him as he refuses to 'belong' to the household of the Heights.

17.

- Lockwood is the first educated character, and he is snobbish about his education, though it appears to serve him poorly when it comes to reading the social signs of the community he is visiting.
- Nelly, who is self confessedly a 'poor man's daughter' nevertheless corrects Lockwood: 'You could not open a book in this library that I have not looked into, and got something out of also' (p. 63).
- Cathy's education of Hareton: Brontë depicts Cathy as both generous and unkind (a true mix of both houses) in the episode where she is teaching Hareton to read (pp. 301–3).

18.

- Books and letters are typically agents for action in this novel. When Lockwood arrives first at the Heights, he notes 'a few mildewed books' near his bed (p. 19). On these, written over and over, are different versions of Catherine's name. The books, corrupted by damp, form a palimpsest or many layered text which both suggest and withhold meaning.
- After Isabella has eloped with Heathcliff, she sends a letter to Nelly which extends to nine pages (pp. 136–44). In it she questions Heathcliff's humanity; sets out an unflinching account of the misery of loveless marriage for women, having been beguiled by romance; and also describes her desire for a gun.
- Letters form a crucial part of Heathcliff's revenge plot, when he forces Linton to exchange secret letters and books with Cathy (Volume II, Chapter VII), eventually luring Cathy to the Heights where she is taken prisoner by Heathcliff.
- Edgar is described by Nelly as spending too much time with his books when Catherine is dangerously ill.

19.

- Heathcliff is arguably the most ambitious character in this novel, using all his acumen to rise from being a foundling orphan without even a name to call his own, through to being in control of both the Heights and the Grange.
- Catherine can also be seen as being an ambitious woman, in that she marries for social standing and hierarchy rather than for love.
- Hareton is keen to rise from his ignorance and to acquire an education, even if the means of that at times humiliate him.

20.

- *Wuthering Heights* can be seen to operate around a profound absence of mothers: Heathcliff has no mother; Catherine's mother dies shortly after Heathcliff arrives at the Heights; Frances dies in motherhood giving birth to Hareton; Catherine dies giving birth to her daughter, Cathy.
- Nelly Dean operates as a kind of surrogate mother to many of the characters, doling out a rough affection and practical advice.

Section Two: Working towards the exam

1.

- Brontë can be seen to engage with many issues central to a feminist understanding of the world. Her blurring of traditional gender characterisation shows this.
- Catherine is wild, wilful and disobedient, requests the gift of a whip, is physically violent to the other characters. Her powerful statement 'I *am* Heathcliff' also needs to be explored in this context.
- Heathcliff, being disenfranchised, has no property and therefore operates as a Victorian female: he can only acquire power through marriage and strategy.
- The place of women in society is explored through the character of Nelly: she operates as a servant, but has access to more knowledge than any other character, both in terms of formal education and in terms of intelligence about what is really happening.
- Isabella is weak and betrayed by her subordination to the discourse of romanticism. However, unlike Catherine, she bravely flees her repressive marriage and escapes to London. Arguably this can be read as the single most effective act of female independence in the novel.
- Linton is effete and sickly, his power derives from a kind of cunning. He is trapped in the domestic realm, and he is despised for it.
- Edgar is representative of conservative patriarchy. He operates with masculine power, cutting Isabella off when she defies him to elope with Heathcliff. His emotional life is subordinate to his intellectual life, which turns out to be his fatal flaw when he neglects Catherine, whom he loves, to spend time with his books.

2.

- The opposition between passion and reason is central to both novels, in which passion is both sexual passion and violence.
- Jane Eyre operates as a governess, which enables her to be socially astute. She is not 'at home' in the house, she is 'at work'. Nelly Dean can also be seen to operate similarly in her commentary in *Wuthering Heights*.
- The landscape of both novels is important for establishing character. The wildness of the landscape permits a certain rebelliousness of character that would be harder to express in a more mannered novel like *Persuasion*, for example.
- The world of the imagination is important in *Jane Eyre*, offering an escape from privations and underpinning an idea that our authentic lives are enriched by fantasy. In *Wuthering Heights*, books are seen as an escape from the real world, but to detrimental rather than beneficial effect.
- The role of education in the two novels is marked and complex: Lockwood's ostensibly privileged understanding of the world is time and again wrong-footed by its encounter with the wild 'natural' landscape of *Wuthering Heights*. In *Jane Eyre*, Jane's academic talents permit her intellectual parity with Rochester but not social equality.

3.

- Both *Wuthering Heights* and *Mrs Dalloway* can be read as novels which have at their centre the opposition between the conservative restraints of civilisation and the chaos of lived experience.
- In *Wuthering Heights* Catherine's excessive love of Heathcliff results in her loss of sanity and ultimately her death. Even when she is dead, both Heathcliff and Edgar seek to lie with her.
- Clarissa Dalloway's obsession with death is counterposed to her desire to bring people together, and to experience love. She expresses this frequently through books, and references to poetry and Shakespeare. For Clarissa, love is always lost: lost with Sally Seton, lost with Peter Walsh and lost in Septimus Smith.
- Love in *Wuthering Heights* is dangerous and disturbing. It disrupts social order and threatens to destabilise the family. This can particularly be seen in the case of Isabella.
- Both novels seeks to depict the world of the sane and the insane side by side, in *Wuthering Heights* represented by the two houses, and in *Mrs Dalloway* by the opposing stories of Mrs Dalloway and Septimus Smith. In both novels the divisions between these two worlds are portrayed as provisional, flimsy and under erosion.
- The social inability to express love as witnessed in Edgar and Richard Dalloway results in an emotional death for their wives.

4.

- The doubling of names and structural repetitions of this novel disrupt our common expectation that a character will be discrete and individual.
- Catherine's assertion 'I *am* Heathcliff', suggests that her notion of herself is only fully realised in relationship with Heathcliff, that the two are indivisible and psychologically indistinguishable.
- The ability for characters to appear from beyond the grave to affect the action of the novel suggests a disruption of boundaries between characters and events.
- Joseph's character is deeply informed by conventional religion and local superstitions. It is internally coherent but presents as almost 'unreadable' to the primary narrator Lockwood.
- The relationship between Cathy and Hareton seems to echo and repeat that between Catherine and Heathcliff and that between Catherine and Edgar. Brontë uses the device of repetition to encourage us to reflect on how love fractures and reconstitutes itself.

5.

- Conventional religion in the form of Christianity operates as a social modifier in both novels, proposing moral constraint and retributive justice.
- Both novels also offer a view of pagan or pre-Christian connection with the earth that seems more authentic and is closely aligned to magic.
- How the novels deal with death is instructive for our understanding of the role of religion in these texts. In both texts where and how someone is buried is important for their salvation. A proper Christian burial is considered vital for forgiveness.
- In both novels biblical references are portrayed with the understanding of the believer but with the scepticism of the agnostic.
- Both novels posit traditional Christianity as part of the patriarchal world view, and use the female characters of Tess and Catherine to challenge that view.
- The idea of 'natural goodness' which is central to Hardy's depiction of Tess is in direct opposition to the characterisation of Catherine as 'wild' (p. 42) and 'mischievous and wayward' (p. 38).

Part Three: Characters and themes

Section One: Check your understanding

1.

- Inheritance, and how a person achieves status and security is central to the plot of *Wuthering Heights*.
- Heathcliff's intricate understanding of inheritance laws is what permits him to plot his revenge.
- Inherited character traits are also significant in the novel, wherein all the main characters are revisited in the subsequent generation.
- Inheritance also has to do with fortune. Hindley inherits his father's fortune and in doing so overturns Heathcliff's fortune: once a foundling, then a favourite son, under Hindley, Heathcliff becomes little more than an abused labourer.

2.

- Heathcliff is the enigmatic outsider, whose identity is never resolved during the course of the novel.
- He is cruelly vengeful, wilfully sadistic to Isabella and Cathy, and could be considered an anti-hero.
- He has been called a Byronic hero, passionate and sexually intense.
- He rescues nobody, indeed his character is the downfall of all the characters including himself.
- He has also been considered a Gothic hero, having a supernatural air to him and an obsessive relationship with the dead Catherine.

3.

- Catherine is described as strong willed and capable of spending hours out on the moors in inclement weather.
- She twice suffers complete breakdowns inconsistent with her otherwise robust constitution, both prompted by Heathcliff leaving.
- Neither the doctor nor Edgar can quite believe the change in her when she falls ill so suddenly.
- A psychological interpretation would suggest that she is broken away from her self, and that is why she fails to thrive.
- A feminist reading would look at the conditions of her life and suggest that her inauthentic marriage is making her ill.

4.

- Brontë's novel explores and confronts Victorian ideas about masculinity.
- If gentle birth is what makes a gentleman, then Edgar must be considered the epitome of manliness: he is fair, well read and wealthy.
- The Victorians were also admiring of a more rugged, adventuring masculinity as seen in Heathcliff's powerful male energy.
- Heathcliff is described as an 'unreclaimed creature' (p. 102) – even love cannot tame him.
- Linton is frail, weak-willed and selfish. He is frequently described in babyish terms 'sucking a stick of sugar-candy' (p. 279).

5.

- As a child Cathy is 'mischievous and wayward' (p. 38) and will not beg to be forgiven (p. 43). Forgiveness is a major theme of this novel, being the antidote to the 'unquiet slumbers'.
- It is disobedience that leads Catherine to be captured by the dogs at Thrushcross Grange, after she has been running shoeless on the moors. At the Grange she must learn to tame her wildness and become obedient.
- Nelly refuses to keep Catherine's secret, for although, as a servant, she must do as she is bidden, Nelly retains her own narrative power.
- Catherine 'seemed to allow herself such wide latitude that [Nelly has] little faith in her principles' (p. 107), suggesting again the alternative moral code of the novel.
- Isabella leaves to marry Heathcliff against the express wishes of her brother. This act of disobedience marks the beginning of her downfall.
- Cathy disobeys Edgar and Nelly, and climbs over the walls to go onto the moors. This determination to transgress the laws which confine her leads to great unhappiness but also establishes the conditions by which she will succeed in forging her own space in the novel.

6.

- Catherine's love for Heathcliff profits her nothing but cannot be called unselfish since it is a narcissistic love.
- The love between Catherine and Heathcliff can be considered a bold attempt to break the boundaries of the self.
- Isabella's love of Heathcliff is romantic and unselfish but ultimately leads to her greatest misery.
- Cathy's love of Linton is generous and largely unselfish, although she sees it as her means of escaping the confines of her 'loving' prison.
- Cathy's love of Hareton is flirtatious and on the whole sensitive to his needs.
- Edgar's love of Catherine is indulgent but fails to recognise who she really is.

7.

- The conflict between reason and emotion, which is at the heart of the choices Catherine makes in this novel, is what gives rise to its deepest expressions of mental anguish.
- The fact that Catherine and Heathcliff are kept apart by social constraints, although they are soulmates, is what provokes their increasingly erratic behaviour.
- Catherine and Heathcliff can be said to embody the 'divided self' of psychoanalysis.
- Hallucinations and dreams, and the effects they have on the characters also amplify the theme of madness and sanity.

8.

- She is cheerful and quick to amend her actions.
- She is loyal and brave, attacking Heathcliff when she realises she has been tricked and trapped.
- Nelly describes her love as 'never fierce; it was deep and tender' (p. 189).
- She brings a gust of positive energy into the desolation of Thrushcross Grange and later Wuthering Heights.
- Her relationship with Hareton restores to the novel a positive account of love between a man and woman.

9.

- Almost all the characters are violent towards each other and are capable of acts of wanton cruelty, suggesting that these relationships are volatile, physically expressive and unrestrained.
- Heathcliff hangs Isabella's dog in order to punish her for her infatuation with him.
- As a child Catherine is attacked by the Thrushcross Grange dog Skulker and then kept at the Grange until she recovers, suggesting that the boundaries between the two households were even then blurred.
- Hindley threatens to kill Hareton and throws him down the stairs, demonstrating his physical power.

- Hindley attacks Nelly with a knife; male violence against women is a recurrent theme, from Lockwood's sawing of the child's wrist on the broken glass through to Heathcliff's beating of Cathy about the head.
- Cathy bites Heathcliff when he imprisons her and Nelly, and Catherine pinches Nelly and slaps Edgar, suggesting that women were not simply victims of male violence, but were just as prone to violent outbursts themselves.

10.

- If we consider nostalgia to be a strong and sentimental attachment to the past or to a place then it is possible to read *Wuthering Heights* as a nostalgic novel.
- Catherine fails to flourish in Thrushcross Grange because of her absolute dislocation from and longing for the Heights, which manifests itself ultimately as a haunting loss.
- Wuthering Heights represents to Catherine the unadapted, authentic self, unmediated by social pretensions. Her attempt to cross into Thrushcross Grange leaves her profoundly dissociated from her childhood and true identity.
- Nostalgia informs Nelly's retrospective narrative: she has roots and is psychologically attached to her place and her story.

···

Section Two: Working towards the exam
···

1.

- Power is central to our understanding of the novel, and it operates through class, gender, age and narrative control.
- Nelly has the majority of the narrative power: she controls much of the action in the narrative, withholding and divulging information.
- Heathcliff, who arrives at the Heights with nothing, and then loses Catherine to Edgar, has the power born of ruthlessness. Having nothing to lose makes him reckless and cruel.
- Catherine, while having no social power of her own, has the power to torment both Edgar and Heathcliff because they both love her and for different reasons she cannot fulfil that love.
- Edgar, who has the advantage of monetary power and influence, nevertheless lacks Heathcliff's potency and is mocked for it by Catherine.

2.

- Possibly the most striking and memorable quotation from the novel, Catherine's assertion that she is Heathcliff and that they are part of one shared soul suggests a religious connection between the lovers, one that is elevated above mere desire to a spiritual communion.
- It implies that their love is essential and exists beyond the realm of conventional romance.
- It suggests that Catherine has surrendered her unique individual identity to his, and that she is now the embodiment of her love for him.
- She also says that he is 'more myself than I am' (p. 81), which can be read as Catherine's desire for Heathcliff's autonomy and masculine freedom.
- This statement also invites us to pause and question Heathcliff's otherness. If Heathcliff and Catherine are indistinguishable, it becomes much harder to sustain a reading of Heathcliff as a radical outsider.
- Brontë is exploring the limits of selfhood and identity in this quotation.
- It must be remembered that this extravagant claim is made at the very point at which Catherine is consulting Nelly Dean about her decision to marry Edgar Linton. Her inability to see Heathcliff for himself, as opposed to an extension of herself, is

part of the psychological permission she allows herself to make the decision to marry Edgar.

3.

- Lockwood, who arrives as an outsider and our narrator, to find the doors of Wuthering Heights 'locked' (as his name predicted), finds it hard to belong to the environments of both the moors and the Heights.
- The use of natural imagery, especially of local flora to describe character, situates the characters as grounded in their environment. Consider Nelly's description of the reception of Catherine at Thrushcross Grange as 'It was not the thorn bending to the honeysuckles, but the honeysuckles embracing the thorn' (p. 92).
- Heathcliff and Catherine belong to the moors and make their home there, walking the moors together even after death, according to the little shepherd boy at the end of the novel.
- Heathcliff arrives as an outsider but nevertheless is easily assimilated into the landscape of the novel by virtue of his natural wildness and tempestuous nature.
- Belonging to the family is also central as it confers legitimacy and therefore is crucial for inheritance. Who stands to inherit the properties is key to Heathcliff's plans for revenge.
- Knowing where you belong in society is another theme of the novel. Each time one of the main characters attempts to cross the boundary between one house and the next, misery befalls them. Even the narrators Nelly and Lockwood are at the mercy of this principle, although Nelly, being native to the area and servant to both houses at different times, fares better than Lockwood.

···

Part Four: Genre, structure and language
···

···

Section One: Check your understanding
···

1.

- The landscape of Wuthering Heights is typically bleak, hostile and unreadable to outsiders. We first encounter it in a freak snow storm, and it is given to storms, thunder and high winds.
- The landscape is harsh and lends its harshness to the characters, especially to those who love it, who become the ghosts who haunt it: Catherine and Heathcliff.
- The literary Gothic landscape is very isolated, contains ruined buildings and graveyards.
- From the perspective of eighteenth-century neo-classicism, the Gothic was perceived as crude and barbaric.
- The moorland is wide and wild; it is impossible to cultivate or refine.
- A feature of Pennistone Crags is the 'Fairy Cave' which ignites the imagination and desire of Cathy.
- Catherine is buried in an obscure corner of the graveyard in a place already being colonised by the moors.

2.

- Lockwood sawing the child's wrist on the broken glass
- Heathcliff's obsession with laying with Catherine's corpse in the grave
- The dog hanging from the tree

3.

- The use of the pathetic fallacy of the weather engenders a feeling of foreboding in the reader.
- The unflinching accounts of domestic violence create a feeling of fear.

- The fact that Brontë creates an unreliable narrator makes us unable to trust in Lockwood's confidence that he will be welcome and all will be well.
- The casual violence which appears normal at the beginning of the novel foreshadows the terrors that will unfold.
- The hostile landscapes and inhospitable buildings also foster a feeling of discomfort and dread.
- All the dogs in the novel are either dead or vicious.

4.

- The sublime is generally considered a heightened feeling that is elevated beyond reason. It is part of the Romantic aesthetic. It is a useful concept in understanding the love between Catherine and Heathcliff.
- The descriptions of the moors and landscape as both terrifying and beautiful form part of the aesthetic of the sublime.
- The sublime is also generally regarded, post-Wordsworth, as participating in a higher or spiritual consciousness in which the world's cares are lifted by something greater than beauty.

5.

- Nelly is frightened by Catherine's dreams and will not listen to them.
- She encourages us to believe in the power of ghosts to haunt and terrify.
- In direct contradiction to that, she also affirms that the dead lie at peace.
- When Catherine claims she has been haunted during her delirium, Nelly dismisses the idea.
- Nelly has a vision of Hindley as a child which prompts her to visit the Heights.
- When Heathcliff is close to death, Nelly is frightened by him and thinks he is already a ghost: 'Is he a ghoul, or a vampire?' (p. 330).

6.

- Two competing narratives cause us to question the notion that truth is simple and that we can trust the narrator.
- The structure highlights the importance of boundaries in this novel and how they might be broken or transgressed.
- The structure is actually very tight and controlled, which it has to be in order to contain the wildness of the narrative.
- The reader is encouraged to question their own assumptions when the story begins to repeat itself with subtle but important differences.

7.

- This is a novel that abounds in mysteries.
- Where does Heathcliff come from to disrupt the family values?
- Why does Catherine claim she has been 'lost' on the moor of her childhood for twenty years?
- What is the nature of Catherine's illnesses?
- Is true love necessarily destructive?

8.

- As in most fairy tales the mother dies very early on in the story and the children are then at the mercy of an unmediated patriarchy.
- Nelly can be seen as the 'fairy godmother', the benign onlooker who works to try and make good the evil.
- Heathcliff operates as a kind of 'Bluebeard' figure in his relationship with Isabella.
- The novel is a quest for true love, which achieves its happy ending with the relationship between Cathy and Hareton.

9.

- It is isolated and subject to the ravages of the inclement weather.

- It is dark, with secret passages and cupboards.
- It is the site of hauntings and inexplicable events.
- There is a grotesque carving over the front door.
- It is bordered by a few stunted fir trees and 'a range of gaunt thorns' (p. 4).

10.

- The stark choices available to the female characters of marriage, destitution or work, depending on class, show Brontë's thorough understanding of the real political conditions of women's lives.
- This is a novel which is alive to issues of class, poverty and education, as witnessed in an examination of the characters of the two narrators: Lockwood and Nelly Dean.
- Heathcliff's arrival into the family, having been rescued from the streets of Liverpool, is based on true stories following the great potato famine.
- The casual violence that infects all the relationships in both houses, violence which is fuelled by greed, territory, poverty, alcoholism and misogyny, exemplifies Brontë's careful dismantling of the Victorian ideal of the family as the site of domestic bliss.

Section Two: Working towards the exam

1.

- The idea of the 'Chinese box' structure, first put forward by critic C. P. Sanger to understand how Brontë creates her narratives, is that there is a dominant frame narrative which contains all sorts of other stories.
- The frame narrative is Lockwood's (his name suggests it will be a locked box) and indeed we gain very little understanding from his narrative. His frame is one of constant uncertainty and error.
- The sliding wooden panels of Lockwood's box-bed (resembling a coffin) reveal another narrative, the swarming letters of Catherine's repeated and fragmented name.
- Other texts within texts are Isabella's letters to Nelly which provide yet another first person narrative within the frame narrative of Nelly's account, which is within the frame of Lockwood's account. Information is witheld and divulged in shifting ways which serves to establish suspense.
- The complex intersecting of stories and texts means that Brontë never insists on a particular moral or critical response to her characters. We are left to ponder the mysteries in our own hearts and minds, for the main narrators are unreliable guides and each of the characters is partial to their own assumptions and understanding.

2.

- 'Last night I dreamt I went to Manderley again.' is the opening line of *Rebecca*. As in *Wuthering Heights*, the house is a dream house, never quite visible, reached by twisted paths. It is a Romantic riddle, haunted by female ghosts, hidden from view.
- The landscapes for both novels are wild, brooding and vast, and provoke profound joy in the main female characters.
- In both novels, when we are first introduced to the house, we are introduced to it in ruin.
- The ruin of the house in both novels suggests not simply material degradation but spiritual ruin. The house is the site of unrest, and strange and ominous disruptions to our idea of sanctuary and home.
- The descriptions of the landscape are in both novels geared to the emotional lives of the characters, and losing that connectedness to the land is the cause of grave emotional disorder.

3.
- Catherine's famous speech to Nelly 'I *am* Heathcliff' (pp. 82–3) echoes Shakespeare's sonnet 116 expressing the eternal immutability of true love.
- The love between Catherine and Heathcliff does indeed endure 'even to the edge of doom' (line 12).
- Brontë's descriptions of the moors that separate the Heights from the Grange establish the emotional tenor of the action, and provide a suggestive commentary on the quality of love: the landscape is given to storms and harsh weather but also to passages of great softness and beauty. These descriptions powerfully recall Blake's poem 'The Garden of Love' in which love denied, curtailed or confined by religious or social convention is corrupted by death.
- Brontë's enigmatic proclamations and assertions of love that resist full interpretation imbue the novel with a deep and singular potency, which in its turn has found its echoes in later love poetry, such as Charlotte Mew's 'A Quoi Bon Dire'.

Part Five: Contexts and interpretations

Section One: Check your understanding

1.
- Property laws and laws of inheritance which disadvantage women
- Irish potato famine – leading to foundlings and orphans abandoned on the streets
- Industrial Revolution, exodus from country to city, decline of traditional rural communities

2.
- Position of women in society
- Catherine's marriage choice
- The power of the narrator: Nelly Dean
- Illness and women: Catherine, Isabella
- Freedom and imprisonment: Catherine, Cathy
- Feminine and masculine characteristics: Heathcliff, Edgar, Catherine
- The female Gothic, women trapped in domesticity (The female Gothic was a term first coined by Ellen Moers to refer to work by women writers from the eighteenth century onwards writing in the Gothic tradition. The female Gothic tends to permit the inclusion of women's desires, and challenges conventional male hierarchies.)

3.
- Man of loneliness and mystery
- Proud and vengeful yet capable of deep love
- A solitary suffering figure
- A blend of both villain and hero
- A tortured character

4.
- Death and romance (relationship between Catherine and Heathcliff)
- Horror and love (Heathcliff's desire to get into the grave with the dead body of Catherine)
- Ghosts and the supernatural (Catherine; Catherine and Heathcliff)
- A haunted house (Wuthering Heights)

- Bleak, isolated landscapes (the moors)

5.
- Wealth and financial security as represented by Thrushcross Grange
- Social status: compare Lockwood and Nelly Dean
- Education/lack of it: Lockwood, Edgar, Hareton

6.
- Comparison with *Mrs Dalloway*
- Madness and derangement: Catherine's brain fever, Septimus Smith's trauma
- Marriage versus passion: Edgar Linton, Richard Dalloway
- Importance of time: in *Wuthering Heights* large gaps in time, yet timing strictly important; in *Mrs Dalloway* very short timescale but every moment is significant
- Identity: Catherine, Clarissa

7.
- Isolated landscape, bleak and hostile to its inhabitants – Romantic view of landscape as either picturesque or sublime and uplifting
- Catherine's dream of being thrown down to the moors from heaven – Romantic tradition of depicting the land as a kind of paradise, a godly creation
- Romanticism characterised by emotion and individualism – Brontë's landscapes are places where people experience their spontaneous emotional responses to the land and each other
- Romanticism part of response to tradition of Enlightenment and Rationalism, characterised by a passionate belief in spiritual freedom and creativity – Catherine and Heathcliff's affinity with landscape

8.
- Shakespeare's sonnet 116: love as 'an ever-fixed mark'
- John Wilmot, 'A Song': idea of true love as 'everlasting rest'
- Charlotte Mew, 'A Quoi Bon Dire': 'everybody thinks that you are dead,/But I'
- Tony Harrison, 'Timer': the ring as symbol of eternity
- Louis MacNeice, 'Meeting Point': the poem suggests that the couple share the same beating heart, and that their love defies time, existing in a time and place that is beyond the ordinary understanding of how those terms might operate

9.
- The wicked or wayward child, Catherine, deliberately flouting the laws of the household and the father
- Heathcliff's revenge, carried out in the name of love
- Brontë proposes an alternative or higher order than conventional religion, an order which is transcendent and in harmony with the laws of nature
- Catherine's writing in her Testament, defacing the legitimate script of religion
- Joseph, with his 'vinegary face', a satirical representation of traditional religion

10.
- Dreams: Freud's *The Interpretation of Dreams*
- The absence of the mother figure, and her substitutes
- Identity: the id, the ego and the superego – represented by: Heathcliff (id – primitive drives), Catherine (ego – social, attached to and in partial control of the id), Edgar (superego – civilised social morality)
- Unconscious – a place of dark desires – Gothic elements

Section Two: Working towards the exam

1.

- Ernest Dowson's poem 'Non Sum Qualis Eram Bonae sub Regno Cynarae' explores how passion for a dead lover makes the poet 'desolate and sick' and infects even his contemporary relationships.

- Christina Rossetti's sonnet 'Remember' focuses on the conflict between physical existence and the afterlife, and for the large part of the poem proposes that the death of memory would be worse than physical death, that not being cherished in a lover's memory would be more painful than actual death. By the end of the poem, she sacrifices her need to be remembered to preserve the happiness of her beloved.

- Seamus Heaney's poem 'Punishment' unflinchingly considers the treatment of women under a partriarchal society, and the tenderness of his account of the corpse is a nod to Heathcliff's grisly passion for Catherine's dead body.

- Andrew Marvell in 'To His Coy Mistress' proposes the exact opposite of Brontë's account of true love: that it is important to love while one has the opportunity, for 'The Grave's a fine and private place/ But none, I think, do there embrace'.

2.

- Both novels are daringly ambiguous when it comes to morality. The bad do not get punished more than the good; the good do not get rewarded more than the bad.

- The multi-layered structure of the narratives shifts the perspective in both *Atonement* and *Wuthering Heights*, raising questions about truth rather than answering them.

- The overarching passion, which carries with it the religious notion of suffering, in *Wuthering Heights* becomes the lens through which we are invited to judge all the characters and their motivations. In *Atonement*, as the title itself partly suggests, moral dilemma and the consequent suffering, is at the heart of the novel.

- Both novels are sensitive to class distinctions with regard to acts of violence. Both novelists invite us to consider why it is more plausible that Heathcliff and Robbie are more capable of committing violent acts than Edgar or Paul Marshall.

- *Atonement* plots the growth of Briony's moral conscience in the absence of a religious framework of forgiveness. She spends the novel trying to correct her error and deal with her remorse. *Wuthering Heights* posits that there is a higher moral code than that of traditional religion, and that is to live true to the power of love.

- *Atonement* is a novel which operates around the concept of shame.

- *Wuthering Heights* is a novel where each character is motivated by their sense of entitlement.

3.

- *Wuthering Heights* was deeply offensive to its original readers for is brutal lack of restraint, its wild content and its unflinching critique of traditional morality.

- The central notion of love beyond the grave, which manifests itself in hauntings and even necrophilia, runs counter to the reader's expectations of 'the greatest love story of all time'.

- Transgression of boundaries is a key theme of the novel, an example of the form supporting the content.

- Using local dialect and native idioms against the authoritative discourse of received standard English challenges the idea of what is proper in literature.

MARK SCHEME

Use this page to assess your answer to the **Practice task** provided on page 112.

Look at the elements listed for each Assessment Objective. Examiners will be looking to award the highest grades to the students who meet the majority of these criteria. If you can meet two to three elements from each AO, you are working at a good level, with some room for improvement to a higher level.*

> **Compare the ways in which the writers of your two chosen texts present women's struggle for identity. You must relate your discussion to relevant contextual factors.**

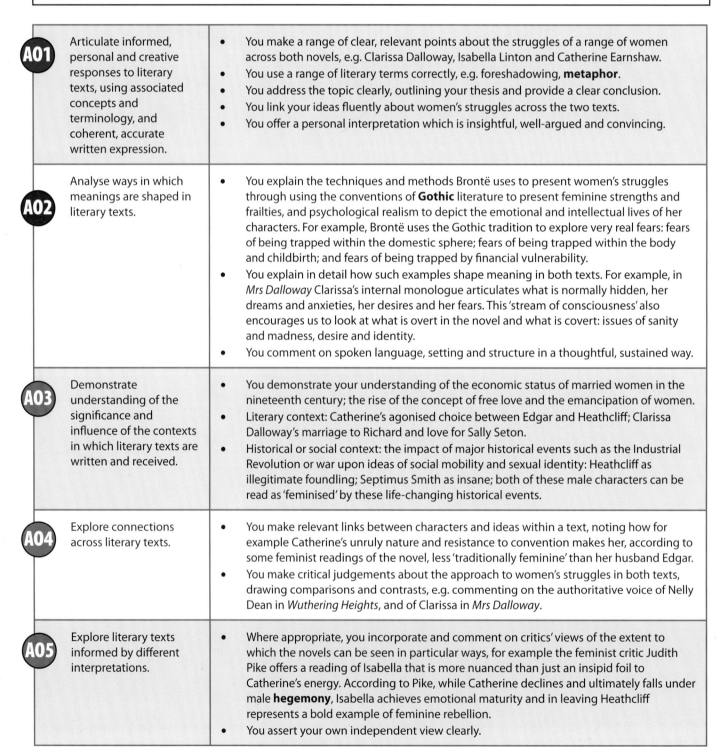

AO1	Articulate informed, personal and creative responses to literary texts, using associated concepts and terminology, and coherent, accurate written expression.	• You make a range of clear, relevant points about the struggles of a range of women across both novels, e.g. Clarissa Dalloway, Isabella Linton and Catherine Earnshaw. • You use a range of literary terms correctly, e.g. foreshadowing, **metaphor**. • You address the topic clearly, outlining your thesis and provide a clear conclusion. • You link your ideas fluently about women's struggles across the two texts. • You offer a personal interpretation which is insightful, well-argued and convincing.
AO2	Analyse ways in which meanings are shaped in literary texts.	• You explain the techniques and methods Brontë uses to present women's struggles through using the conventions of **Gothic** literature to present feminine strengths and frailties, and psychological realism to depict the emotional and intellectual lives of her characters. For example, Brontë uses the Gothic tradition to explore very real fears: fears of being trapped within the domestic sphere; fears of being trapped within the body and childbirth; and fears of being trapped by financial vulnerability. • You explain in detail how such examples shape meaning in both texts. For example, in *Mrs Dalloway* Clarissa's internal monologue articulates what is normally hidden, her dreams and anxieties, her desires and her fears. This 'stream of consciousness' also encourages us to look at what is overt in the novel and what is covert: issues of sanity and madness, desire and identity. • You comment on spoken language, setting and structure in a thoughtful, sustained way.
AO3	Demonstrate understanding of the significance and influence of the contexts in which literary texts are written and received.	• You demonstrate your understanding of the economic status of married women in the nineteenth century; the rise of the concept of free love and the emancipation of women. • Literary context: Catherine's agonised choice between Edgar and Heathcliff; Clarissa Dalloway's marriage to Richard and love for Sally Seton. • Historical or social context: the impact of major historical events such as the Industrial Revolution or war upon ideas of social mobility and sexual identity: Heathcliff as illegitimate foundling; Septimus Smith as insane; both of these male characters can be read as 'feminised' by these life-changing historical events.
AO4	Explore connections across literary texts.	• You make relevant links between characters and ideas within a text, noting how for example Catherine's unruly nature and resistance to convention makes her, according to some feminist readings of the novel, less 'traditionally feminine' than her husband Edgar. • You make critical judgements about the approach to women's struggles in both texts, drawing comparisons and contrasts, e.g. commenting on the authoritative voice of Nelly Dean in *Wuthering Heights*, and of Clarissa in *Mrs Dalloway*.
AO5	Explore literary texts informed by different interpretations.	• Where appropriate, you incorporate and comment on critics' views of the extent to which the novels can be seen in particular ways, for example the feminist critic Judith Pike offers a reading of Isabella that is more nuanced than just an insipid foil to Catherine's energy. According to Pike, while Catherine declines and ultimately falls under male **hegemony**, Isabella achieves emotional maturity and in leaving Heathcliff represents a bold example of feminine rebellion. • You assert your own independent view clearly.

* This mark scheme gives you a broad indication of attainment, but check the specific mark scheme for your paper/task to ensure you know what to focus on.